SOUL MASTERY JOURNEY

THE MYSTERIOUS NATURE OF THE DIVINE

JULIA LEWIS

RITZ
BOOKS

Soul Mastery Journey: The Mysterious Nature of the Divine

Paperback ISBN: 978-1-960460-90-5
Kindle ISBN: 978-1-960460-00-4

Published by RITZ BOOKS
A Division of Steph Ritz LLC
Cover design, author headshots, and graphics by Steph Ritz

Dedication

To all of the Benevolent Beings who are working with me to assist humanity in achieving Soul Mastery and Spiritual Sovereignty.

And to Richard, for your love and support
(Dec. 21, 1946 - Nov. 5, 2018)

"I love you neither with my heart nor with my mind. Just in case the heart might stop, the mind can forget.
I love you with my Soul.
Soul never stops or forgets."
~Rumi

Hindsight is 20/20

As you read this book, you will find it is not in chronological order. Some of my experiences, like pieces in a jigsaw puzzle, didn't fit or make sense until years, even decades later. I've tried to tie them all together for you.

You can probably relate in your own journey how the puzzle pieces of your life experiences can take years before they finally fall into place.

I have been on a treasure hunt since childhood, without a map to follow, collecting gems along the way to fill my treasure chest. Unknowingly, my Soul and my Spiritual Lineage have guided me because I never lost the ability to clearly hear them. I was also able to use the mastery skills I was born with to navigate the obstacles I encountered.

I use the analogy of jewels and a treasure chest because the most valuable thing you will ever have is the ability to fully access and seamlessly use your Soul's Mastery skills to succeed in making the world a better place with your unique contribution.

Hopefully my story will help you to relate to your own non-linear journey of awakening to your Divine Purpose and how your Soul came prepared for it.

Table of Contents

Why Me? – Can You Relate?

What does it mean to be a Soul having a physical experience? To Know Thyself?

In my search to understand myself, someone recommended I explore astrology, numerology, and other systems based on my birthdate. These experiences led me to psychic and past life readings on the more esoteric side.

Blending the intellectual pursuit of my mind with the wondering inspired by my Soul led me to listen to the invisible and explore my Spiritual Nature.

There is an army of unseen Benevolent Beings surrounding me. They are a resource to help me to stay on course with my Soul's Mission. Communication is one of my Soul's Masteries. I have a natural ability for making analogies to translate concepts in a way that helps people to more easily understand them. I'm a good listener and get intuitive hits or insights as I listen.

The further down the rabbit hole I go…the more I am in awe of just how awesome every one of us is! We have a personality that, for the most part, has absolutely no idea about the masteries our Souls have achieved. Shakespeare said "we are merely actors on a stage".

So true!! What role am I playing in this improvised movie in this lifetime? I get to make suggestions to drive every scene. I can refuse to take part in the scenes that don't fit me. I have choices, even when bullies try to convince me I don't.

The absolute last thing I ever thought I'd be doing in my "retirement years" is bringing this body of work forward.

In reality, though I didn't know it at the time, I had been preparing for over 20 years! Memorial Day weekend of 2000 I had a rafting accident. I was thrown from the raft and hit my head on a rock. Time stood still. I could see the murky water and feel the slimy green moss on the cold rock.

I silently asked if I was dead... I was not the least bit afraid. I was in a place of wonder.

I wasn't consciously aware of and didn't know for years, until I explored with my guides, that in that life changing moment I had a near death experience and made an agreement to take on a new Soul Mission. I had accomplished what I came to do. I could leave...but chose to stay.

As I popped up to the water's surface, I felt the strangest feelings in the area of my brainstem - I could feel it mending back, like a zipper being pulled up. I also hit my shin really hard on a rock and I could feel that mending as well. I got two black eyes and a terrible whiplash, but I healed up.

After the rafting accident, I made a dramatic shift in the focus of my study of energetic healing. I immersed myself and mastered a variety of healing methods. Usually, I'd study for 2 or 3 years taking numerous courses for a specific healing technique, often reaching the level of a qualified instructor. I wanted to understand the why and how of influencing a person's energy field for both good and bad. To understand why some are more receptive or easily influenced. I wanted to get past the blame/shame and help people get well.

Perhaps a happy side effect of my choosing to not drown in that rafting accident is the raft guide doesn't have to live with the guilt of misjudging the current and colliding with the rock which catapulted me out of the raft.

I've learned that the people interested in what I offer are the ones who have explored the more esoteric systems of spiritual self-development. I'm in the deep end of the esoteric, spiritual, personal development pool. They don't have to agree with me, I'm not going to try to convert or convince anyone. If this makes sense to someone, then they are willing to walk the plank of the unknown.

I think of Indiana Jones where he had to take a leap of faith into that canyon only to find himself supported on a seemingly invisible bridge that takes him safely across to the holy grail.

My leap of faith is trusting my Benevolent Beings (BBs) to assist me to walk side by side with the Soul Army committed to inspire humanity to raise its vibration and expand its Spiritual Consciousness and Sovereignty. Our group effort is making it easier for people to say yes to a higher purpose.

I believe that a good analogy for what I've done with developing the Soul Mastery Journey is like a rockhound who kept digging in a cave.

After years of exploring and determined digging, they found a huge meteor. It turns out that it is the most valuable stone ever found. This Galactic gift benefits humanity in a way that no other Earthly stone does. It is valuable to the segment of humanity ready to use it.

In the Galactic realms, I have the ability to gain information and perspective around an individual's possibility and their obstacles to accessing that possibility. I also have the ability to remove these crippling obstacles.

The Soul Mastery Journey opens your inner set of eyes and sheds light on your Soul's Mission and the obstacles blocking your success.

My audience is the people searching to understand their Soul's Mission - people who are ready to remove all of the obstacles preventing them from using the abilities their Soul has already mastered, so they can accomplish their current mission.

My role is to do an analysis specifically for you. The analysis is to:

1) List your Soul Mastery Skillset for your current mission

2) Explain the obstacles preventing you from accessing this Mastery

3) Energetically remove the obstacles.

4) Connect you with your Spiritual Lineage

5) Activate your Spiritual Sovereignty

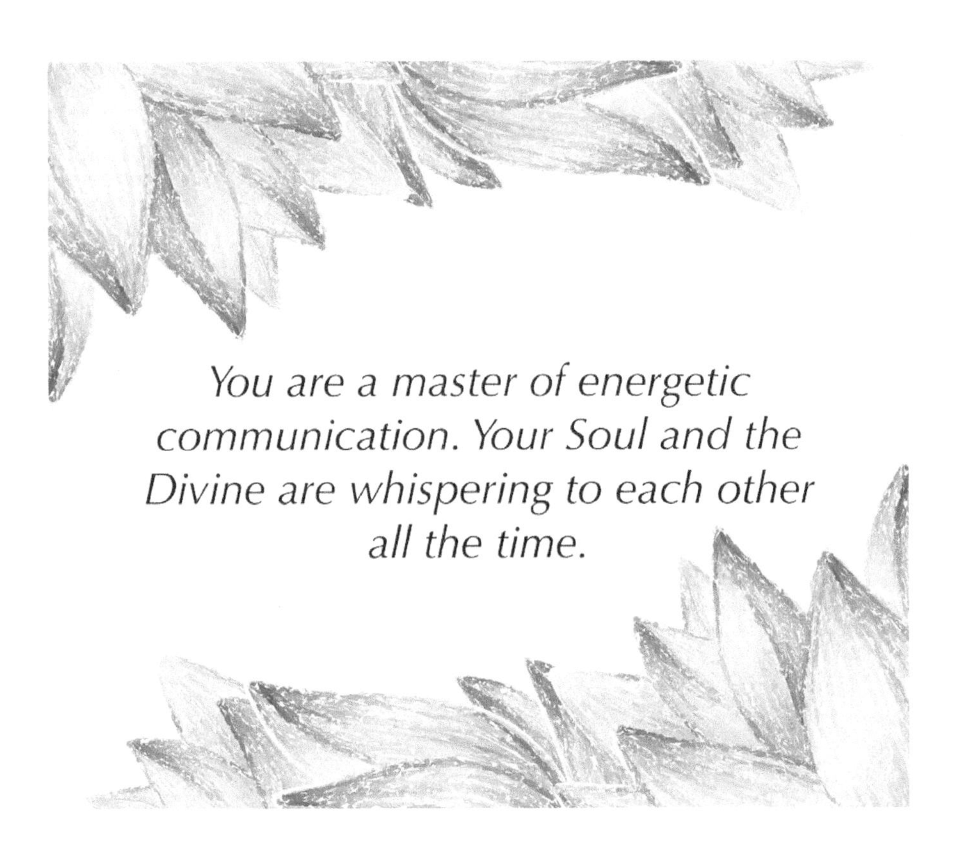

Recognizing this and removing the obstacles to this communication enriches your experience and impact in the world.

A powerful love resides in you. It flows stronger than all of the waterfalls on Earth combined. It shines brighter than the Sun and all of the stars in the heavens.

The Mirror

When I look in the mirror, I see a reflection that is opposite to what others see. Not that many others ever see the real me. The body suit I'm wearing is just the vehicle. The real me is the driver. I am still sometimes guilty of confusing my identity by what I observe, rather than by trusting that inner voice that whispers who I really am.

When I catch a glimpse of myself in a reflective surface like glass or water, I notice my appearance and tend to shift into identifying with it; when in fact my self-reflection could drive me deeper into my self-discovery.

Can you relate to the land of misfit toys? Being rejected because you didn't fit in? Forming friendships with the other misfits because the cool ones didn't want to be your friend? Watching other kids get special attention from the teacher and get passed over or picked on? Being the last one chosen for teams? Was your glass half empty or half full? What do those people really know anyway?

Having two sets of eyes has been a lifesaver. One set is turned outward and the other inward. Survival dictates that I must conform and mirror other people's behavior to fit in. Cultivating my connection with, and awareness of, my inner abilities has been a long slow journey.

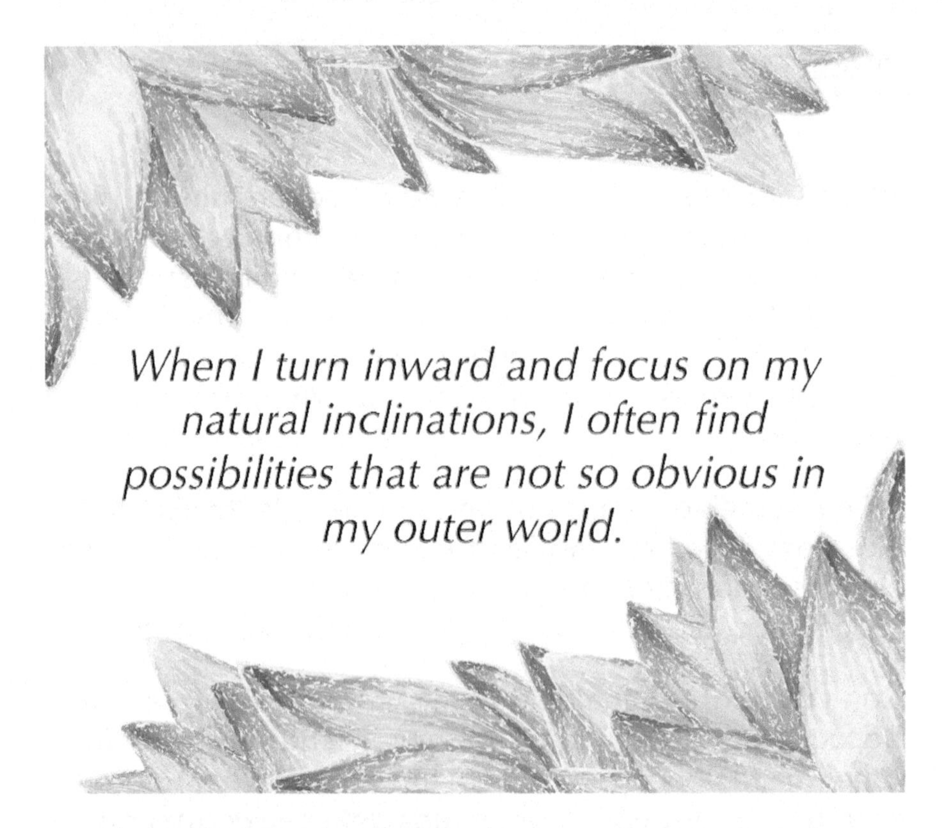

Remembering to use my inner eyes to help me navigate is one of my superpowers.

The Soul Mastery Journey awakens your inner set of eyes. What do you see in the mirror?

The Soul Mastery Journey

Life is a journey of awakening. Some can see through the veil and remember who they are and use the skills their Soul has mastered over its many incarnations. The inner voice urging from within is the shining beacon of light radiating from the Soul.

Using the analogy of a driver in a car. The vehicle is the physical body, and the driver is the Soul. How interesting that mankind is making driverless cars; mirroring the lost connection of the Soul with the physical body.

Giving up one's autonomy and allowing themselves to be controlled by external means is also a crime against humanity because it enables disempowerment and imprisonment for everyone.

Ascension is the process of awakening to your Divine Nature. The Divine, or Creator of all that is, flows through every Soul to experience and achieve mastery.

Awakening is much like going through school. As you ascend through each year of school, you acquire competence that builds as you go. Your Soul is unique in its expression, inclinations, gifts, and talents. Your inner voice pushes you forward to awaken to your Divine Nature.

In my awakening journey I was fortunate to attend several seminars by the witty personal development speaker, Jim Rohn. He is known for his razor-sharp one-liners. One that hit me like an arrow is "How long are you going to spend in first grade?" Clearly you can't stay in first grade and ever expect to achieve mastery.

Julia with Jim Rohn

Awakening for some is like seeds planted in fertile soil. They bloom so easily. While others have a much more difficult journey, as if planted on poor or rocky soil. Your inner voice is lovingly pushing you forward.

Humanity has awakened in consciousness over the history of time, only to be dragged back down into the darkness of separation from their Divine Nature. The Earth dimension is one of duality. Duality lends a very complex terrain to navigate. It appears as a battle of Good vs Evil, polar opposites with only one side able to be victorious. The opportunity for a Soul to incarnate in a place of duality is actually a very high honor.

There is a battle of the dark forces and the light forces. The code of ethics is far different for the light and the dark. The dark has no respect for the autonomy or free will of your Soul. It conspires to trick, deceive, manipulate, and undermine your Soul's Mission by seducing your mind to the "dark side".

The dark impersonates the light.

They come with messages of hope, cloaked in an energy that corkscrews into their victims to pull them into the dark. The dark forces manipulate you using your dreams and desires as fuel. They try to shift your focus to have/achieve any and everything you desire. They will seduce you with all the "shiny objects" of the world if you aren't careful.

Awakening to your Soul's Divinity is not an intellectual

pursuit. True awakening requires surrendering to the Divine before you can have your obstacles to the Divine removed. You could achieve this via prayer, turning it over to a higher power. You can do personal spiritual development work to release all the reasons you hold on to the obstacles.

I've been working with client's emotional obstacles for over 25 years, overcoming fears of:

- Public speaking, flying, dying
- Taking tests, interviews
- Meeting new people, heights, elevators
- Spiders, snakes, dogs
- Being in relationships, leaving relationships
- Driving after an accident
- And all kinds of other fears

As I deepened my communication with my Benevolent Beings (BBs), they told me I should start working with the Sacred Lotus. I had heard that name about 6 months before. I had a client come to me to explain a problem she was having.

I asked my BBs what was going on with her. They told me that in a previous life she stole energy from the Sacred Lotus and was cursed for doing so. If she were to return that energy to the Sacred Lotus, it would remove the curses. She chose not to do this, so I'll never know.

I was a bit nervous about meeting this Sacred Lotus as I didn't want to offend it and risk getting cursed. My BBs told me the Sacred Lotus was a much higher-level Spiritual being than they are. It exists in the 7th plane of existence.

I had to google the "7th plane" since I had never heard of it before. It is defined as *the plane of the Creator of All That Is, the highest plane of existence. On the Seventh Plane, we can utilize the energies of all the planes without being bound by any oaths and commitments to them. This is because the energy of the Seventh Plane creates the other planes.*

https://www.healyourlife.com/what-are-the-seven-planes-of-existence

My BBs told me that the Dark Forces managed to shut off access to the Lotus shortly after Jesus left his body, and They replaced it with Pagan rituals and Religions. These Dark Forces infiltrated Religions to create fear of the "life after death" and a vengeful God to control people. Religions then taught salvation could only be achieved by compliance. Compliance made it so much easier to control people and further separate them from their Divine Nature.

The Sacred Lotus is an amplifier of the Divine's complex frequency. Via resonance, your Soul's messages can more easily be heard.

The Sacred Lotus is like the Sun. It is powerfully bright and its warmth cuts deep passages into the individuals who sit before it. These passages are like cutting holes in a box - the box of duality, the box of lies that hides your true nature - so you can breathe more easily.

With practice, the grace of the Sacred Lotus drills so many holes in the box of lies, that you awaken to your Divine nature.

When I met the Sacred Lotus, I saw this beautiful flower sitting in a pool of water. Its radiance captivated all of my senses. It was ecstasy to be in its field. It took me months before I could be in its presence without feeling woozy. I was told this pool of water holds the power of the Lotus. If an individual were to go into the water, they would soak up powers and be punished for eternity for doing so until they returned the power.

The Sacred Lotus makes it possible for me to restore your Soul Mastery and Spiritual Sovereignty when I work with you on your Soul Mastery Journey.

Learn more:

www.soulmasteryjourney.com

The Soul's Journey

Your Soul is the conduit for, among its many names; the Doer, the Divine, the Creator of all that is, the love that animates and expresses through all beings.

Using the analogy of a car: Your Soul climbs into the vehicle (a body) and drives it. Your Soul is also a vehicle of the Divine. The Divine is the energy that flows through your Soul. Your Soul whispers instructions to your body on how to drive the car.

Your Soul has a mission - a destination with various experiences along the way. Your Soul chose this vehicle (body) as it was the one that would best serve your mission, even though you may not have all the features to easily accomplish your mission.

In this analogy, the car has a mind of its own that comes preprogrammed with all the history of its manufacture (DNA, cultural and societal influences, etc.) that create strengths for your Soul to succeed in its mission and weaknesses to overcome. Your Soul also has to override any negative experiences that happen to you along the way. The car (body) has the "free will" to decide if it will take instructions from your Soul or not. This is where your personal work is needed when there are any obstacles to your Soul's voice being heard and acted on.

One of my clients was born into a family lineage of many curses. These curses created obstacles for their Soul's Mission. They suffered with anxiety, doubts, fears, and negative self judgement.

My assessment:

There are 4 curses in their family line. 3 on the mother's side and 1 on the father's. All four are active.

The mother's family line had dominion over other families. They exploited these families and caused unnecessary suffering. This went on for at least 3 generations. Over these generations the oppressed plotted to retaliate. One of the oppressed was able to make curses that penetrated the mother's family line.

The oppressed used a form of sorcery to curse the descendants to suffer as they were made to suffer. They locked these curses very tightly into the field of my client's ancestors.

The curses on the mother's side:

1. The descendants will lose their power and become the oppressed. They will struggle and no matter how hard they work to climb out of their pit, they will slide back down and their spirit will be broken.

2. The descendants will perpetuate their despair, stealing joy by exaggerating all that they fear.

3. The descendants will yearn for what they will never have. All that they yearn for will be taken away.

The father's family fought in a resistance to tyranny. The oppressors used sorcerers to scare the freedom fighters.

The curse on the father's side:

You will always have to fight tyranny, no matter how many battles you win. You will always be a victim of tyranny.

After clearing these curses with the guidance of my BBs, my client felt much calmer and more empowered. The negative judgements and fears declined significantly. They now have more confidence and peace of mind. The crazy weird things that happened to their parents, grandparents, aunts, and uncles all made sense by understanding the curse's influence.

Another client had all kinds of personal and family drama and health issues. Their mother had Multiple Sclerosis for over 50 years. One of the sisters was stuck as the caregiver. This sister resented this role and suffered because she felt like she was a prisoner and unable to travel. Another sister was a professional, but she injured her back and suffered with back pain and would have numerous episodes of being laid up in bed. My client had health issues that made them miserable. Then there was the brother. The brother struggled in his career, causing his family to suffer due to the financial stresses. His wife became ill. She ignored the symptoms until it was full blown cancer. She refused treatment and suffered terribly before dying a painful death. My client came to me distraught in the final stages of their mother's life. The caregiver sister had turned mom over to the brother as she needed to care for one of her adult children. The mom's health took a sudden decline when she was moved to her son's home and was suffering excruciating pain.

My assessment:

Each member of the family made a Soul agreement to suffer for the brother's benefit. His Soul's Mission is to know what it would be like to see the people you love and care about suffering all the time. The role the mom, siblings and his wife agreed to play was to suffer illness and pain for his Soul's experience.

What an incredible gift of love from his mother to suffer with MS for over 50 years. The loving commitment for both his mom and wife to die horribly painful deaths right in front of him. The love of his siblings to suffer for his benefit as well.

I explained this to my client that in order for their suffering to stop the only option they had was to rescind the Soul agreement made with their brother...which they did.

Soul agreements aid a Soul's Mission. The Divine has so many things it designs into your experience.

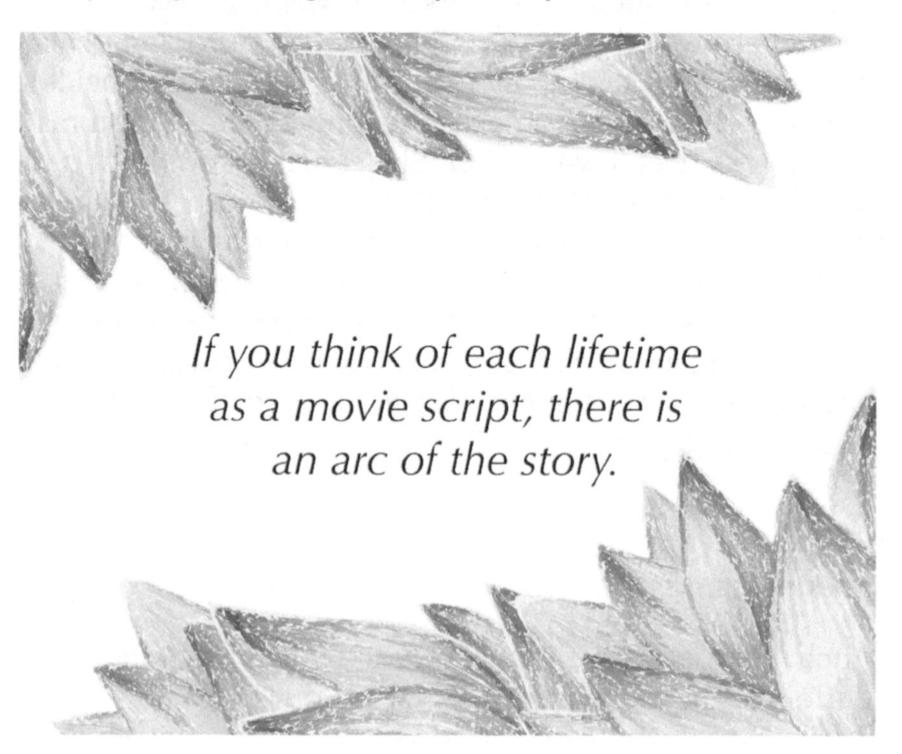

There are challenges, villains, heroes, victory, defeat, struggles, tragedy, joy, happiness, suspense, a roller coaster of emotions that can have a happy or sad ending. Some actors in your movie could win an award for their role, maybe even you.

One of my Soul's Missions was to experience the ultimate violation of being cheated on, seduced, and manipulated by lies and deceit that violated my trust as well. You'd think it would be easy to find someone to agree to it. I went through several relationships before I found the guy willing to do it. I met him at church. You'd think that is a place to meet someone nice! He seemed like a good man - successful in business, charming and available. He was going through a divorce because she decided she wanted to be with a woman. I knew them both and had her blessing to date him. Long story short, he was never committed to me. He cheated on me from the beginning, I was just too blind to see it. Two psychics told me that he was "the love of my life".

Then one day he left me a voicemail. He told me that he was in Europe with another woman and that we would have to redefine our relationship to just be friends. This is the man I took to the airport and was supposed to pick up on his return. For 3 years he had promised to take me to Europe on one of his business trips.

I was more than devastated. I felt like something had been ripped open in me. I remembered how Jesus tore down the curtains in the temple when he was upset with the way the moneychangers were violating the Temple. With every ounce of my being, I let go a powerful message into the thought field that this kind of behavior was wrong. This was in 1997. My explosive message added fuel to the collective thought field to help women and men find their voice. To make a boundary against this type of violation.

One of my Soul's Mastery Skills is the ability to communicate. While my mind has no comprehension of this, I'm told that with the proper fuel I can launch a piercing message into the thought field we are living in. The realization in 1997 of how deeply I was violated was the rocket fuel to deliver this crucial message. While I didn't know it until recently, this betrayal created an extraordinary energetic explosion. He definitely won the Oscar for best performance by a liar, cheat, and deceptive con artist.

Looking back at your own journey, can you relate to having to overcome or deal with intergenerational trauma? Have you experienced glass ceilings or roadblocks to achieving your dreams? Do you feel like your life has purpose, yet struggle to figure out what it is?

You are not alone. Because you recognize and can identify your struggles, you are searching for answers. If you are interested in exploring your own Soul Mastery, I invite you to continue reading to learn more.

Waking up inside the dream

Do you aspire to describe this dream you find yourself in here on Earth? You are a co-creator as well. In the Indiana Jones movie, *Raiders of the Lost Ark*, Harrison Ford decided to rewrite one of the fight scenes. It was scripted for him to have hand to hand combat. Since he had dysentery and was too sick to fight as scripted, he decided to use his gun and shot the bad guy instead. He created a better scene.

You see through a prism of your belief system, the universal thought field and every other thing that influences your perception. I can only describe what I see, what I'm shown and what I've experienced. Perception can be like a huge disco ball with millions of mirrors reflecting light.

There are many millions of points of view. This is mine:

In my first 50 years I didn't know much about my Soul, my Soul's Mission, or my Soul's Mastery. I learned early on in Sunday School the concept of having a Soul. It was the part that went to Heaven when I died. In my teens, I learned it was the part that went to hell if I was bad. I didn't give my Soul's role much thought until I started communicating with my BBs. I was too distracted with living my life.

My first career started when I was a Senior in High School. It began with a job at a local TV station working in television studio production. Three years later I made my way to work for NBC in Washington DC. I loved it. An absolute dream-come-true. When I was 29, I went to a Chiropractor for the first time.

Something inside of me woke up.

It urged me to go to school and become a Chiropractor myself. I was torn because I had a great career, dream job and lived a comfortable life. I took the leap of faith. I became a Doctor of Chiropractic at the age of 36. The same something urged me to move to California, start a new life and explore this new world of opportunity and possibility.

Within my first year of practice as a chiroprator, I was introduced to energetic healing. I was using the techniques I learned from NAET allergy elimination. I just followed their formula and got mixed results. I wasn't alone, other practitioners had similar experiences. Other techniques sprung up using a different spin. NAET itself was a spin on someone else's energy techniques.

I found myself taking at least one seminar a month, immersing myself in learning the various nuances of this energetic way to reprogram the body. I learned more ways to ask questions of the body to figure out how to help. I called myself a Body Detective. I helped people overcome autoimmune disorders, food and environmental allergies, and break free from the effects of emotional traumas.

I wanted to better understand this complex machine of the human body. I spent over 2,000 hours in a Chiropractic Neurology program that my gut told me didn't have the answers I was seeking. Surely the secret was in the neurology of the body, but wait - what about all the emotions and their influence? I abandoned that program.

I spent the next two years learning an energy healing technique that said I had to get in an altered state of consciousness and connect with something outside of me to access healing.

I didn't know why, just that something inside me told me so. I kept searching.

Next stop, I found a philosophic body of work that explained how energetic healing worked. It held the missing piece of why I struggled with energetic healing methods.

Unfortunately, this philosophy had a missing piece itself because it credited all success to the power of the mind. I do give it credit for paying more attention to my Soul. The philosophy said I'm a Soul in expression and that I'm ever evolving. With these understandings I came to know that the thing inside me that urged me to look further is my Soul.

Looking back, I agree with the saying, “When the student is ready the teacher appears”.

In 2012 I ended a twelve-year, long-distance relationship. I was sidetracked into staying with an emotionally, physically, and financially draining relationship. By the summer of 2012, I had good communication with my guides. The previous three years were extraordinarily hard. During that time, I’d ask my guides about leaving the relationship.

They’d say, “Stay.”

I wish I had figured out sooner to ask, “Why should I stay?”

I was desperate to get free of being dragged down by the destructive nosedive his life had become. I begged my guides to let me leave.

I finally asked, “Why do I have to stay?” I waited for their answer, it didn’t come instantly. I kept asking.

One day a voice whispered, “Because you think it’s your job to fix broken people.”

Those words shocked me. It was like I was struck by lightning. My reply was “Nobody is broken and if they were broken, it is NOT my job to fix them!” I made the call and ended the relationship.

Even though I broke up with him, I was afraid of him. He had a very strong vindictive streak. I could feel his anger, like a red-hot poker that made me afraid. I lived in fear he would show up and hurt me. I didn’t feel free until a little over a year later when he died.

I turned inward to find myself again at age 56. I reflected on the choices I had made. I was determined to get centered in the truth of who I really am and what I'm here to do.

Reflecting back, my mom introduced the possibility of reincarnation and past lives...that scenario seemed possible. In my 30s I started exploring new age teachings that focused on the power of the mind, not much about the Soul. Something inside me said to keep looking. Most of the teachings revolved around how to manifest. I went from praying to Jesus who would answer my prayers, to a philosophy that I had all the power to use my willpower to answer my own prayers.

I did affirmations and visualizations, but somehow, that just didn't seem right to me. One of the teachings introduced the concept of the evolution of consciousness. I could relate since I was always learning something new and my understanding was certainly evolving. I then became curious about the Gurus from India. Maybe meditating and their philosophy would expand my understanding of myself.

I was at a group meditation where they played a song I'd never heard before. My tears started flowing and I couldn't understand why it made me cry. How could some people singing three words make me cry so uncontrollably? The chant was Om Namah Shivaya. It still makes me cry. Translated it means "I Bow down to Shiva". Lord Shiva is the most powerful of the Hindu Deities. Om Namah Shivaya means bowing down to the quality of Shiva in each of our consciousness.

Hearing this chant dramatically changed the direction of my life.

I searched “Om Namah Shivaya” on YouTube. I listened to several versions, but nope didn’t have the right energy. I found a version by Krishna Das. I felt like Goldilocks - it was juuuusssstttt right! I listened to it over and over again. I googled Krishna Das, and to my surprise, he was a white guy from Long Island. I saw on his website that he was doing a retreat on Maui with Ram Dass in 4 weeks. I checked my points with American Airlines - was able to book a flight, flying first class. I registered for the retreat with full intentions of spending the day sightseeing and listening to Krishna Das every evening.

When I arrived at the retreat venue, I found the pavilion where the music and teaching was to happen. On the stage was a huge picture of an Indian man wrapped in a blue plaid blanket. The picture had the most calming influence. Apparently, he was very important. Something he did propelled Ram Dass and Krishna Das on their life’s journey that made this retreat possible.

Honestly, I knew nothing about Ram Dass. Maybe I had heard his name...but didn't know his story. The retreat started that evening with Krishna Das singing his chants. I was new to this type of call and response singing, but it felt good to do it. I anxiously waited for him to sing "my song". Since he didn't, I stood in line to ask him when. He told me tomorrow night. I was so psyched...it was like Christmas was going to happen the next day.

Even though I went for the music, I was curious what this retreat was all about. I decided to sit in the back and take it all in. Surprisingly, Krishna Das walked in from the back of the room and sat down next to me. Now what are the odds of that? He could have sat anywhere. He did this for 2 days straight. I didn't say anything to him - I was being respectful. Another interesting coincidence (like there ever are any) I met KK Sah who was a child growing up with this great Saint pictured on the stage. I was impressed by the stories they shared about this man in the picture who they called Maharaji. That seemed like a strange name to me. They also said that his formal name was Neem Karoli Baba. Now that seemed familiar - I decided to call him Baba.

Even though I had planned differently, I only went sightseeing one day. I attended morning to night in a sea of excited devotees of the Saint in the blanket who died in 1973. The last day was the grand finale. This was when Ram Dass would touch each attendee, one by one, and give a blessing of his Guru, Neem Karoli Baba. There was so much excitement, people lined up like it was a big Black Friday sale. Krisha Das and his band sang a Hare Krishna chant as each person bowed before Ram Dass to receive their special blessing. I waited in the back, observing people's reactions. I could see that something really cool was happening. After about an hour, I finally had the courage to get in line.

Ram Dass had a stroke, so he had only one strong hand and he had it wrapped in a brace. The routine was bow down and he'd touch your head. My turn came. I bowed down. He touched my head. I felt nothing. I was surprised by my own reaction. I lifted my head up against his hand, like a baby goat bumping its mom for more milk, and he blessed me again. This time I felt something in my forehead actually pop. I was blissed out. Whatever that was, was awesome!! No wonder everyone was so excited!

I went back home to California with an experience that slowly unfolded and brought me to where I am today. I had a connection with the man in the blanket. I knew he was my Baba. I continued to listen to Krisha Das. I didn't feel a connection to Ram Dass, yet loved hearing his stories about his Maharaji, my Baba. I continued exploring a couple other Gurus, who are alive, because I knew there had to be more to the connection they had to the Divine.

When I was young, I went to Sunday School. I was fortunate that they taught me that Jesus loved me. That Jesus performed miracles. If I prayed to him, he'd answer my prayers. I felt really close to him. I'd even scoot over and sleep on half of my twin size bed so Jesus had a place to sleep next to me. Of course, I'd wake up in the morning rolled over on Jesus, but he didn't seem to mind.

Ram Dass and Krishna Das told stories of Neem Karoli Baba's deep love and respect for Jesus. It took a man in a blanket to remind me of the Jesus I knew and loved as a kid.

My Worst Nightmare

When disaster strikes: is it a blessing or a curse?

There is a Chinese parable about a farmer and his horse. Somewhere along the way I heard this story. It stuck with me and I share Alan Watts' version with you now:

Once upon a time there was a Chinese farmer whose horse ran away. That evening, all of his neighbors came around to commiserate. They said, "We are so sorry to hear your horse has run away. This is most unfortunate."

The farmer said, "Maybe."

The next day the horse came back bringing seven wild horses with it, and in the evening, everybody came back and said, "Oh, isn't that lucky. What a great turn of events. You now have eight horses!"

The farmer again said, "Maybe."

The following day his son tried to break one of the horses, and while riding it, he was thrown and broke his leg. The neighbors then said, "Oh dear, that's too bad," and

the farmer responded, "Maybe."

The next day the conscription officers came around to conscript people into the army, and they rejected his son because he had a broken leg. Again, all the neighbors came around and said, "Isn't that great!"

Again, he said, "Maybe."

The farmer steadfastly refrained from thinking of things in terms of gain or loss, advantage or disadvantage, because one never knows... In fact, we never really know whether an event is fortune or misfortune, we only know our ever-changing reactions to ever-changing events.

Eastern Wisdom, Modern Life: Collected Talks: 1960-1969 Paperback – August 18, 2006 by Alan W. Watts (Author)

https://www.amazon.com/Eastern-Wisdom-Modern-Life-Collected/dp/1577311809/

https://youtu.be/byQrdnq7_H0

For the past 20 years I've felt that there was something bigger for me to do. I would develop and teach some kind of method or technique that would help people overcome the obstacles blocking them from achieving their life purpose or mission.

The Divine ramped up this plan in 2018. In April, my landlady decided to sell the place I had rented for 14 years because she could sell at the peak of the real estate market bubble. I was happy for her, but felt devastated for myself. Rents had skyrocketed as well. I had 60 days to seriously downsize.

A week or so after my landlady's notice, I was handed another devastating blow. My friend Richard, who is like a brother to me, was diagnosed with colon cancer. He lived 3,000 miles away on the East Coast.

As much as I wanted to help, I couldn't because of my living situation. I had 1100 sq ft of furniture and a lifetime of treasures, books, clothes, etc. I gave at least 80% away...and I still had too much stuff. I was in a tailspin on where to move. A friend had a room in her house to rent, but it wouldn't be available in time.

As the deadline for my move became uncomfortably close, I reached out to friends for a place to stay. Fortunately, at the last minute my California mom and dad invited me to move in with them. I met Connie in church when I first moved to California. I became a part of their family, spending holidays and family celebrations with them for more than 25 years. They had extra room and were happy to have me around.

Whew...dodged that bullet...just in time. By July, I was all moved and starting to relax. Remembering the parable...was my situation good, bad or maybe?

I was getting used to my new routine, commute and living situation. Richard was completing his chemo and radiation and seemed to be turning the corner. Near the end of August, he invited me to fly out to visit him in Maryland. I was his power of attorney, so I helped get him caught up with paperwork. I returned home. Two weeks later he took a dramatic turn for the worse. He had to go into hospice. On September 11th I flew out to help. I canceled all of my Chiropractic clients indefinitely. Thankfully my home situation was in good hands, I didn't have to worry there. The next eight weeks were grueling. Until you experience helping someone you love go through hospice, you'll never know how physically and emotionally demanding it can be.

At the five-week mark my mom, who lived in Texas, had a stroke. She was in ICU. After a week it became clear that she was not going to recover. I couldn't leave Richard, so my brother and sister took care of my mom. Now I'm in shock. I've got two people down. Richard tanks and hospice moved him to their care center. He was all drugged up and fading away. It was a Sunday morning. The nurse called and said today would be the day. I rushed to be by his side. At noon my brother called to say that my mom had died. I then realized that I would lose them both on the same day. I sang Dolly Parton's song, "I will always love you" over and over to him as I held his hand. It was a day I never thought I'd ever experience. When he took his last breath, I was amazed at how quickly his lips lost their pink color. How different his body felt. I knew it was just his body that died. I fantasized that his mom, dad, and my mom were there to greet him when he crossed over...but who really knows what happens.

I left the hospice center and returned to the house we bought together 40 years ago. Many things were in the exact same place I left them when I moved to California in 1992. I was his sole heir. The Maryland house would go to foreclosure because he leveraged it to pay for the house I inherited in Virginia. In 2001 he took me to the Virginia property and shared his excitement for his plans to build. He started the house in 2007 but never finished the inside. Like the Chinese farmer...was this good, bad or maybe?

It became apparent that I'd have to close my office in California. My office lease was up for renewal in March 2019, so it was perfect timing. I had to spend so much time on the East coast, I couldn't be there for my patients. Just when I thought I had things under control, the Divine hand had more up its sleeve.

I was cleaning up after the contractor when my phone signaled a heart-breaking text. My California mom, Connie, died unexpectedly. It was only one week until I had a plane ticket to return in time for Mother's Day. In my big empty house, I screamed as loud as I could until I was hoarse. The tears wouldn't stop. How could I lose her? She was my only mom left.

The grim reaper wasn't finished. My Aunt, who seemed vibrant and healthy, had a heart attack, and died without warning two weeks after Connie died. In June my dearest, 92-year-old friend died as well. I was a puddle on the floor. The tidal waves of loss knocked the wind out of my sails. I still had to deal with Richard's estate, the two houses and my California life. I couldn't be like the Chinese farmer....it was all bad. Loss after loss after loss had taken its toll.

The Rose and the Thorns

It had been a month since Richard died. With other things under control, it was time to see the house in Virginia. It is a very unconventional, contemporary design. Two octagons with a rectangular great room between them. The walls are lined with huge 3'x7' windows. The vaulted ceiling was lovingly covered with tongue and groove pine by Richard's hands. He completed the ceiling and put tile in the three bathrooms. There were toilets, but the water wasn't turned on. No flooring, no ac ducts, no overhead lights, no kitchen.... just bare walls. I had considered selling it as is, but people wanted to low ball me since it wasn't finished. I decided it would sell for a better price once completed.

I had never seen the house plans or discussed the design with Richard. I was not prepared to make all of the interior design decisions when the original builder started back working on the house, only months away in the spring. I was flying by the seat of my pants, with my hair on fire. I found myself sitting all alone in this 6,000 sq ft empty house, trying to figure it all out. Looking back, I honestly don't know how I did it all.

I discovered the house had a very unique energy to it. I'd sit and listen. My Guides explained that it was a portal. A portal to what? I listened more. Soon I could sense there were Benevolent Beings surrounding me. I was shown that I could travel to other portals to meet other Benevolent Beings. Kind of like hop scotching to other universes or dimensions. This house was like a galactic cell phone tower that connected to other galactic cell phone towers so I could communicate with some really cool Benevolent Beings. I started calling them BBs for short.

It seems that the BBs I met had a special interest in me. They wanted to help me to help others with their Soul's Mission. Those Benevolent Beings clearly wanted to be a part of the mission I was stepping into. I hadn't figured out the details of my mission and was hoping they would let me in on it. I asked them to work on me, but they could only do it when I was physically in the Virginia house. Over time, the portal started connecting to me when I was in Maryland working on the estate. Then the connection expanded and was able to connect with me in California. It was an interesting experience.

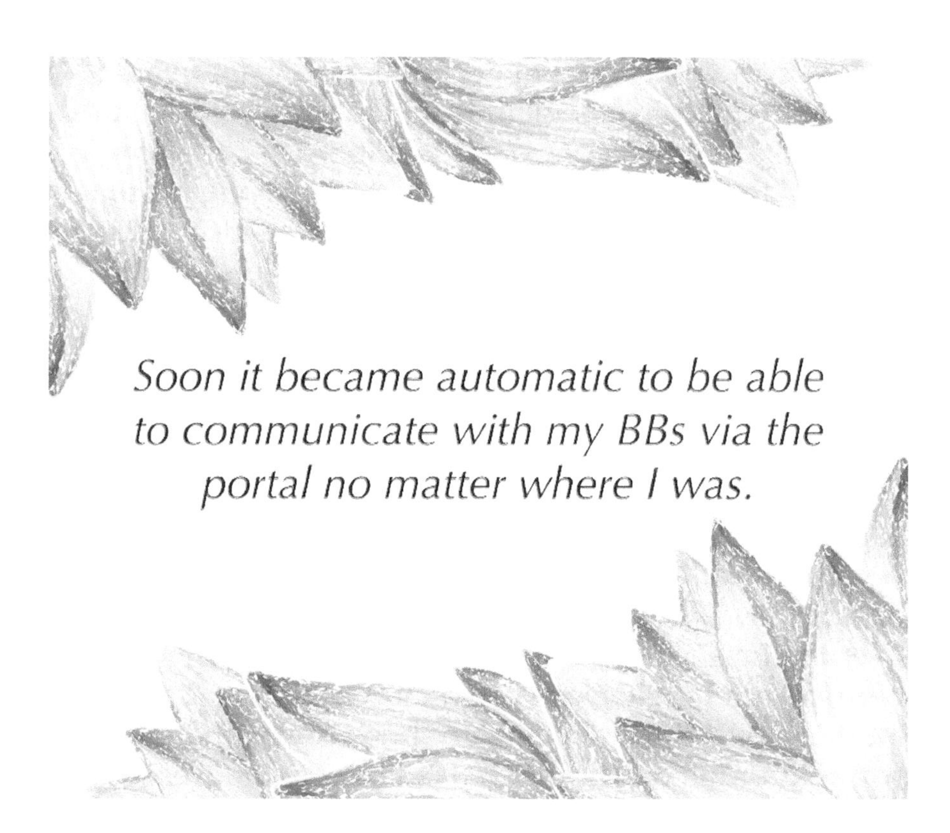

This house and property are strategic for my Soul's Mission. In 2000 I was in a rafting accident. I was thrown when the raft was upended by some strong rapids. I hit my head on a rock. Time stood still. I could feel the moss on the cold rock and the water was murky....it was so peaceful and still. I wondered if I was dead... I then popped up out of the water. I felt the strangest thing in my upper neck...it was like my brainstem was fusing back together. When I went to get out of the water, I could feel my shin repair itself. I was injured and could have died, but somehow, I didn't. In 2001 Richard bought this property. Somehow, he knew this was the perfect location for my next chapter.

My world took a sharp turn in a new direction after that near-death rafting accident. I started that 12-year, long-distance relationship. I immersed myself in learning a variety of energetic healing techniques to the point of qualifying to teach each one I studied. I explored my Spiritual Nature and connected with the loving presence of Neem Karoli Baba, the Indian Guru who also influenced famous creative people like actress Julia Roberts, Apple's Steve Jobs, Ebay's Jeffrey Skoll, Google's Larry Page and Facebook's Mark Zuckerberg.

https://en.wikipedia.org/wiki/Neem_Karoli_Baba

Richard started building the Virginia portal house in 2007. He seemingly lost interest in completing it, became ill with cancer, leaving me a house that I could finish exactly how I wanted it. 2019 was the year of getting over the finish line to earn the coveted occupancy permit. That magic piece of paper was awarded on my mother's birthday...it couldn't get any better than that! I sorted through and emptied the Maryland house. I closed my office in California. The roses of victory had many thorns due to the loss of the people I loved so dearly. It became clear that my journey was leading me to move to Virginia. The sharpest thorn of all, I lost the life in California I spent over 25 years to build. The Divine hand continued to slam every door except Virginia.

Synchronicity and the Paranormal

I've lived in a variety of cities and houses before I inherited the unfinished house in Virginia. At first, I was so devastated by my grief that I'd just sit in that big empty space and try to wrap my head around the job ahead of me. I sent out a cry for help to the universe...asking for support. Support came in surprising ways.

The builder who built the shell 12 years before still had all the plans and was willing to complete the job with me. At a time when builders were busy, he was available. Because he was the original builder and because I inherited the house, the county saw me as an original owner. This made it possible to reopen the building permit under the less restrictive 2007 rules, instead of having to conform to the current rules.

The county is known for being very strict. The woman in charge had a reputation of being unreasonably demanding and ruled with an iron fist. I started calling her the Queen of Permits. I sent her love every day for the 9 months it took to get the house ready to be inspected. My neighbors warned me that she would make it extremely difficult. They were convinced her department had it out for anyone in our little community.

The builder's plan was to get the house ready to be inspected before asking to reopen the permit. His strategy was to show her that we really did mean to cross the finish line. Richard had promised her department that he would complete the house 3 years before his death. My builder wanted me to demand that she reopen the building permit and send out an inspector. I instead wrote a letter acknowledging Richard's lack of keeping his promises to her and her department. I explained his illness and death. (I knew that her business side couldn't punish Richard anymore - he was dead. In fact, her compassionate side might feel sorry for me and the mess he left.) I asked for her permission to reopen the permit and to show my sincerity, I requested an inspection. Every word was filled with love. I treated her with the respect she deserved.

The Queen of Permits did make us jump through some small hoops, but they were easy compared to what she could have done. My neighbors were in disbelief at how I was able to get the Queen to go so easy on me. I didn't visualize or try to manifest manipulating her. The power of sincere love goes a long way. It also helps to have the Divine hand guiding the way.

Looking back at my life's journey I can see how the Divine had created so many synchronous events. As a Chiropractor, I had the opportunity to practice the art of energetic communication. The definition of Chiropractic is that it is a philosophy, science and art. I understood the basic philosophy that the power that made the body heals the body. There is an innate intelligence or wisdom of the body that makes healing happen. The science part is the attempt to explain how people get such good results with Chiropractic. Then the art piece.

The magic in any profession is the result of the art of the individual's way of doing things. Mechanics who can seem to fix anything. Musicians who create symphonies and melodies, are able to sing and play instruments with such precision. Artists who use their imagination and skill to create masterpieces. Inventors who tap into ideas and then bring them into form.

The art of Chiropractic is the part I didn't learn in school. They pointed to it and tried to explain it, but in reality, it was my unique expression.

The beauty of this profession is there are a variety of ways to treat from very gentle to very forceful. I was drawn to the gentle, more energetic ways. One day, about halfway through Chiropractic school, my knee locked up in class. I couldn't stand. My classmates carried me to the clinic.

One of the Doctors there had a reputation for doing high force adjusting. I was afraid of his style. I also knew that the procedure for unlocking my knee required a high force correction. I had total confidence he could do it. I also knew in order for him to do it, I'd have to completely relax my body and trust. In the moment that he set up the procedure, I pushed past my fear and gave him total control of my leg. He felt my trust and he so precisely set my knee back in place that I've never had a problem since. It really hurt and tears shot out of my eyes, but I experienced the art of the blend of energetic and physical connection based on my trust and his love. That was a great teaching moment for me and my classmates....and maybe him too.

Being in the right place at the right time requires perfect alignment and timing so all the dominoes can smoothly fall.

My parents often had disagreements that escalated to physical violence. When I was 4 years old, my alcoholic dad started beating my mom. She yelled at me to take my 2-year-old brother out of the house and go get help.

We lived one house away from a busy street. I walked to the corner and I could see a police car at the drive-in hamburger place catty-corner across the street. I looked both ways and made it to the other side with my little brother in tow. I vividly remember looking up at the officer as he was eating and said, “My dad is hitting my mom again.”

I’ll never forget the look on his face. He turned to his partner in disgust. He told us to climb in the back seat. I clearly remember him asking me, “I don’t remember where you live, could you please remind me?"

We made the short drive to my house and they broke up the fight. My parents gained a new respect for how resourceful their little girl could be.

Is it normal for you to be in the right place at the right time? Can you relate to all of moving pieces it takes for that to happen? Is it really "normal" or just "normal for you"? Just like they said in the TV show, *A-Team*. "I love it when a plan comes together."

Who am I?

Since you are reading this book, this is a familiar question. Maybe you can relate to my attempts to answer it. Ultimately, I believe I'm a Soul having an experience in this body. I often wonder, am I on a lunch break playing a game in some other reality?

Is any of this real? Who knows, I'm playing along.

I've been in this body for over 65 years and I've held many identities or roles so far. When I was maybe 8 or 9 years old, I had a very peculiar thought for a kid that age. I was pondering the Jack and the Beanstalk story. There was a giant at the top of that beanstalk. What if we were just a speck of dirt under the fingernail of a giant? Maybe that was my Soul's way of letting me know that we here on Earth are a very small part of a much larger whole.

While wondering, I've contemplated many things about myself, you too? I've taken numerous courses, classes, and trainings to get deeper and broader perspectives, you too? In my teens there was a TV program called *The Gong Show*. Panelists would hit a big metal gong if they didn't like the amateur's performance. To me, the visual of someone hitting a big gong was the epitome of letting someone know they were way off base. As I've pondered what really happens when I die, what if there are no Pearly Gates or Hell? What if I enter a room with somebody hitting that big gong? What if there is a different possibility? What if we interpret through our belief system lens and see/experience accordingly? I laugh to think a Big Gong could possibly await me.

After my grandfather died, I could feel his energy in my field. It was like he had come to me for help. One of my friends was a dowser and dealt with disembodied energies (Souls). I asked her to help me. Her dowsing told her to send my grandfather's energy to some level of Purgatory. Years later I learned how to guide disembodied energies (Souls) to the light. I remembered my grandfather being sent to Purgatory. I went looking for him there and helped him go to the light. Why should he be stuck there, just because her belief system sent him there?

A friend of mine was an avid atheist. My curiosity got the best of me so I went looking for him when I heard he had died. He was hiding in the dirt somewhere. I asked him what he was doing there. He said, "I'm dead what do you think?" I said, "hey if you're dead, how can you be having a conversation with me?" That changed his tune. I gave the long spiel of how someone could go to the light after they die. He decided he'd try that. About an hour after I ushered him to the light he returned. He told me "you are right," and he went on his way.

Another friend died...I went searching for her. She was with her family unit hanging out in no man's land. I told her the spiel and she went for it too.

I've experienced this enough, that I do believe I can go to "the light" and get the opportunity to go somewhere new and do something different. I didn't give much thought to what the Soul might take with them as it experienced an incarnation. Even after 18 months of establishing communication with my BBs in the Virginia portal house, I never wondered if my Soul had more to offer me in this lifetime.

It was interesting when they decided to tell me. I was attending a three-day online workshop. One of the assignments was to describe your audience, the people you serve. I asked my BBs to help me figure it out. I was amazed as their words spilled out onto the paper. My audience is people whose Soul has mastered what they are here to do and all they need is to connect with and surrender to this inherent mastery.

Inherent mastery? My Soul has a toolbox of mastery skills and I could use these tools to make it easier to get my Soul's Mission accomplished? That concept made me very curious. I asked my BBs to tell me more about how I could help people learn about their Soul Mastery Skills. They described how Soul's achieve Mastery and are able to bring this ability along with them to accomplish their current mission.

My job would be to a) inform them of the specific Mastery Skillset they brought for their current mission b) explain the obstacles preventing them from accessing this mastery and c) energetically remove the obstacles. I could see that I already had the ability and skillset to help people that way.

I Wish I Knew Then What I Know Now

Consciousness, the Sea you live in, is very dynamic and influences you, whether you know it or not.

Scientists have discovered that humans are far more resilient than they once understood. Neurology uses the term plasticity to describe the ability to bounce back - like when you push on plastic and it deforms, it has the ability to regain its shape. Epigenetics describes how your interaction with your environment influences your genetic expression. The double slit science experiment concluded the observer influences the observed. The four-minute mile is an example of one person daring to break that glass ceiling, and once they did - others did too.

I love Isaac Newton's quote "If I have seen further, it is by standing on the shoulders of giants." One of my requirements for physics was taking calculus. My Calculus professor looked like the super handsome movie star Omar Sharrif.

He inspired me with his way of making the formulas and word problems relevant. He had a great sense of humor. One day he was dressed in black -he told us he was in mourning for the Algebra class after ours because they did so poorly on their exam. What a hoot! He was regularly voted best teacher by the student body.

I struggled with the calculus concepts and would go to his open study time and he patiently led me through the thinking process. I was the only one with an A in the class. I studied hard and had super prepared myself for his final. My one sheet of formulas had every scenario I could think of.

As I stood in the hall waiting for the door to open, a classmate said he heard from the class last semester that the professor didn't make people take the test if they were happy with the grade they had, that was his test strategy. Hmmm...

Once we were all seated for the exam, the professor told the class, "Julia has the only A. She is excused from taking the test. The rest of you get to take it."

Part of me wanted to take that test since I'd studied so hard. Thankfully, I gracefully accepted his invitation and left. I couldn't help think about that poor guy who didn't study... I wonder if he was happy with his grade?

My Calculus Professor taught me more than math. He taught me about caring. He modeled going the extra mile.

His example taught me how to connect with people and inspire them. So many wonderful qualities rubbed off on me. When I read Isaac Newton's quote, about 3 years after my calculus class, the first person I thought of was him. Had I understood consciousness, I would have seen the connection of his influence sooner. He is a Giant I'll never forget and be forever grateful for.

Scientists observed electrons behavior in the double slit experiment. Electrons! Electrons were influenced by the observer. Hmmm... If electrons are influenced, they must have a relationship with that Sea of consciousness as well. WOW...What if every electron in your body is influenced by your conscious and unconscious thoughts, your genes, your body's neuroplasticity, and resilience?

In 2007 I was driving on the highway and hit a pothole. The car jolted causing me to bounce in my seat. The oddest thing happened. My back started hurting. Long story short, that rapid compression herniated a disc in my back. I couldn't walk for a month. I learned first-hand what a 10 on the 0-10 pain scale really feels like.

One of my Chiropractor friends had recently taken a course and was using what she learned to help me get back on my feet again. It had to do with giving a "healing suggestion". Thankfully, Chiropractic treatments prevented me from needing surgery and within a few months I was able to take the "healing suggestion" seminar she took.

The technique is called Zone Healing. It was developed by Dr. Thurman Fleet, a Chiropractor in San Antonio, Texas. He started in the 1930s with the body of work he called Concept Therapy. Zone Healing was the way he used the philosophy of Concept Therapy as a Chiropractor. Funny, I was born and raised in San Antonio. My mom knew about Dr. Fleet and Concept Therapy. I didn't find out about it until I had a brush with disaster and was helped by his technique.

I traveled from California to Texas and the East Coast, every month for two years to study this expansive body of work created by Dr. Fleet. I even became certified to teach it. He created a chart that explained how "the observer" affects "the observed". This chart diagramed how a Dr's "healing suggestion" bypasses the Patient's conscious mind and directly influences their unconscious mind.

This golden nugget, describing how a "healing

suggestion" could possibly work, explained a lot of the phenomenon I had already observed in my 15 plus years of Chiropractic practice.

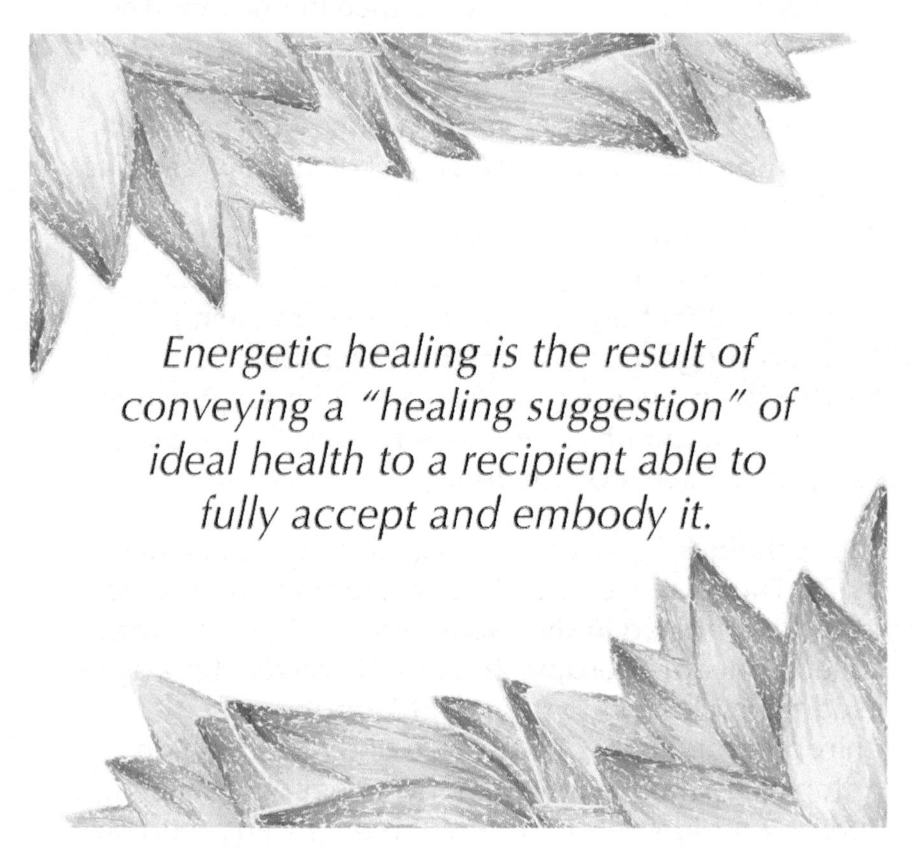

What matters more than any technique is harnessing trust, hope, and faith to more strongly influence a healthy outcome. I wish I knew this when I was a student in Chiropractic College.

The Long and Winding Road

They say the journey of a thousand miles starts with one step. They never said how there would be twists and turns, setbacks, plateaus, wind at my back pushing me along and headwinds forcing me to dig deep to push through. My journey has been filled with helping hands, kindness from strangers, and synchronicities. I've experienced victory more often than defeat, yet the defeats sharpened my resolve to resist giving up or settling for anything less than my heart and Soul yearned for.

I had my first astrology reading soon after I started my Chiropractic career. I was curious what the stars might have to say about me and my future. The only thing that I clearly remember was he told me that I had lived a charmed life. Me? Really? He must have missed all the despair, struggle and loss I had pushed and pulled myself through to get to the new beginning that laid before me.

I am the oldest of four. My mom dumped a lot of the responsibility for caregiving my sister and two brothers on me. We were only 18 months apart, but I had to step up to be the adult by age 7. Once she convinced my abusive, alcoholic father to leave, she was a single mom. She struggled with her own cesspool of insecurity and trying to make ends meet to provide for us kids. Her mother, my grandmother, would give us a helping hand, but at the price of shaming, judging and manipulation. My mother was the oldest of three at a time when first-born boys were prized. Even though she won a beauty pageant at the age of 3, her mother squashed her dreams while praising her two deadbeat sons.

When I was 13, my grandmother did the unthinkable. My mom was struggling to pay all the bills with her teaching job, so she tried moonlighting with sales. She was selling a contraption that was supposed to help big truck engines improve gas mileage. Somehow my Grandmother convinced a psychologist my mom was crazy because she was selling this contraption. This psychologist pretended to be a customer and because he had no knowledge of this device, he decided my mom was certifiable crazy and signed the papers to commit my mom.

I stayed home from school one day to help my mom get caught up at home while the other kids were at school. I went outside to put out some trash and was surprised to see my grandparents and a Sheriff preparing to spring their trap. I believe the Divine knew what was going to happen that day and wanted me to witness firsthand just how evil my grandmother could be. I watched as this Sheriff dragged my mom away. She was taken to the mental hospital on South Pressa. This was back when a family member could have you locked up for pretty much any reason.

My mom was truly a fighter. She knew she wasn't crazy.... that my grandmother had fabricated a story to have her locked up and take her kids away. Back then the psychologists had all the power. Just like in the movie "One Flew Over the Cuckoo's Nest," resistance was futile. My mom kept fighting and they kept giving her shock treatments. She stopped fighting when they hit 25. 6-12 are the standard. She didn't deserve to have even 1. Us kids had to move 150 miles away to go live with our grandparents who crushed their own daughter's spirit and self-confidence many years before. My job quickly shifted to defending my mom and comforting my devastated siblings.

I wish I could say that my mom regained control of her life, but the system pigeonholed her as "mentally ill". Disturbingly, every time my mom would try to get a job, my grandmother would go running to the employer and tell them how my mom had been in the mental hospital and my mom would get fired. It didn't take long until my mom quit trying and became dependent on government disability. I have never figured out what my grandmother's power play was all about. However, this event did line me up to be in the right place at the right time for my career in TV which came 4 years later.

I was a prisoner of my grandparents too. My brother and I signed up for a paper route. It gave us some spending money and more importantly something that prepared us for leaving home. My job was collecting the money. I'd go door to door. One of my customers had a really cool pink, convertible sports car. The lady who lived there was friendly when I'd knock on her door to collect. One day I asked if she had any children. In my world, that is what females did. She smiled and told me that she didn't have children and that just because she was a woman didn't mean that she had to have children. WOW! The first time I had ever heard that I had a choice!

I went to summer school every summer during 9-11th grade. I knocked out a bunch of my required classes, so by the time I reached my Senior year I only had 3 classes to graduate. We lived in the poorest side of town, so it was common for students to have jobs too. I had a friend who landed a job working at the local ABC TV station. I caught the bug... I wanted to work in TV too!

I interviewed at all 4 stations. Surprisingly the PBS station told me directly that I'd never get a job because I was a female! That didn't stop me. The only station that gave me any hope was the NBC affiliate. I called the supervisor every Friday at the same exact time for a good 3 months asking if there were any openings yet. One Friday he asked if I could start Monday! It was the 3-11pm shift. I could ride my bike there and my grandfather would pick me and my bike up and take me home.

This job led me to meet Richard and qualify me to get my dream job at NBC in Washington, DC. Along the way to DC was a stopover in Birmingham, AL because Richard was offered a good job there. It wasn't easy for me to get a job in TV there. That made me depressed and feel like life wasn't worth living. It sounds crazy, but it was sheer agony to have to work at a department store, then a Country Club restaurant kitchen making salads. I interviewed, but nobody was hiring in TV. I'd slip into thoughts of, "I'd rather be dead." I never devised a plan, I just wanted to die. At age 21, the only reason I had for living was my little poodle, Princess. I knew Richard would carry on...but I couldn't leave my Princess.

Wishing I could die is a recurring theme, even up to today. I read about the people who jumped off the Golden Gate bridge and survived with numerous internal injuries and broken bones. I figured if I drove off a cliff, I'd end up totaling my car, breaking some bones and still survive it...so why bother...tough it out. Somewhere along the line I heard the phrase, "wishing I was Bambi's mother." Oh yeah, that was a cute way of saying I wish I was dead. Sometimes my journey ahead seemed so steep I wanted to hit the eject button. While I have friends who say they never have wished they were dead...I find it hard to believe life has been that easy on them.

The depths of my despair have pushed me forward.

Once I made my mind up that I wanted something, the long and winding road would take me there. The course that weeds people out before pre-med is organic chemistry. It was incredibly hard for me too. One of my co-workers said it knocked him out of trying for medical school. I hung in there, and somehow pushed through it, along with all of the other courses in Chiropractic College that forced me to dig deep to pass them. Every final exam and National Board exam it took to earn my Chiropractic Diploma, graduating Cum Laude, and the coveted license to practice in California was worth every sacrifice. All the hope and tears that pushed and pulled me on the long and winding road only to find out that I had lived a “charmed life”.

Discernment

My journey of seeking answers, perspective, and wisdom led me into the world of communicating with the voices of energy beings because I had seen other people doing it. Some call these energy beings Guides, Angels, Ancestors, Saints, Spirits, Messengers, Guru, Jesus, God, the Holy Spirt and I'm sure many other names.

I use the term Benevolent Beings now to describe the wide variety of loving beings who are offering to help me in my Soul's Mission. When I was a child, I prayed to Jesus. I could relate to Jesus the son and God the father. I was confused about the invisible Holy Spirit that looked like a white bird, yet trusted it was important and valuable to me.

Prior to going to Chiropractic school, I hung out at an herb store. The owner used muscle response testing to determine if a supplement was appropriate. She had a little study group where I learned about "talking to guides" for answers to my questions. They described how I could get into a prayerful like state and ask for my guide to talk to me. When one appeared, I could ask their name and any questions I had. It seemed easy so I went home and tried it.

Sure enough a voice appeared. I asked its name and it said "Beelzebub". I was shocked, as I knew that was another name for the Devil. I immediately called the lady in my study group, terrified that I had summoned Satan! She told me to light a candle and tell it no thanks, I want to talk with a guide that Jesus sent.

The next voice that appeared told me his name was

Horace. In my mind's eye he looked like a Roman soldier. He was my invisible friend, who went to Chiropractic college with me. He had a very calming influence. He always knew if I passed a test. My focus in school was to learn as much as I could and most importantly, pass my tests. Having Horace to talk to gave me confidence because he helped me overcome my self-doubts.

Once I graduated, I packed up a Uhaul and drove cross country from Atlanta to California. One day, about halfway through the trip, I started talking with Horace about my next adventure. He told me that it was time for him to leave and he wouldn't be talking with me anymore. I was devastated. My constant energetic companion and trusted guide was leaving me. I'd have to rely on my own intuition now.

I didn't ask for another guide. I had more confidence in making my own decisions. Once in California I met more people who used muscle response testing, pendulums and dowsing to get their yes/no answers. I also had a good sense of which answers were "in alignment" rather than my desires influencing them.

My instructors who used dowsing and muscle response testing stressed the importance of being in a neutral state when asking a question, otherwise I could override the correct answer. I found that my answers were only as good as the questions I asked. I could only get a "yes" or "no". This is no qualifier option of "yes, but." Muscle response testing and dowsing are very black and white tools in a world that also has many shades of gray.

Channeling is another way of connecting with energy beings. This requires a bigger commitment. Rather than just ask questions and get answers, you allow your body to be a vehicle for these voices to speak through you. I met a woman who channeled Merlin. I was fascinated by how her appearance and voice changed when Merlin was speaking through her. She described how it was a relatively simple thing to do. I followed her instructions and sure enough, a voice came through. Remembering my experience with Beelzebub, I wanted to be the conduit for a heavenly presence rather than hell.

I connected with a group of beings who called themselves the Cherubim Angels. I invited small groups of people over to my house once a week and the Cherubim would come through. At first it was words, then they shifted to singing. Each Angel had its own unique energy. They were sweet and powerful. People said the channeling sessions gave them answers for their questions or insights that brought them peace. After doing this for about a year I decided that I didn't want to be the vehicle for someone else's message. I decided that they could just get their own body. I quit channeling.

I started listening to people's energy field and asked specific yes/no questions. My premise was the field that surrounds us holds the answers. In working with patients, I would ask specific questions of their field, with the purpose of restoring harmony and function. I had a flow chart that would help me to determine what area to focus on.

I'd start with structural misalignment, then check for emotional causes, then move to miscommunication in the organs and systems of the body. My goal was to restore proper communication which led to restoring proper function. I found the emotional component required deeper listening. I had a list of types of emotions, which would help me narrow down the category. This method of questioning helped the patient to get in touch with the situation/s that played a role in their current problem.

My patients became consciously aware of the emotions that drove their pain. One of my patients would come in with neck pain and she'd ask, "Who is the pain in my neck this time?"

Another of my patients had rheumatoid arthritis. Her journey started with analyzing her immune system and pathogens. It didn't take long to uncover the emotions in her childhood that created the opportunity for this inflammatory condition. The beauty of the arc of her treatment was her personal relationships dramatically improved and the inflammation decreased significantly. Even twenty plus years later, her hands still show the deformed joints of the arthritis, but she has no pain or heat that originally brought her to my office.

Sometimes I'd hear emotions that I didn't want to repeat to my patient. How could I tell them that they felt like they didn't deserve to live? I took the leap of faith and told them and they broke down crying, agreeing it was true. Their silent struggling with their emotional pain was causing body pain. By naming the elephant in the room they were able to address the underlying cause and heal physically and emotionally.

My intuition deepened and improved every day I worked with patients. I found that I could better energetically match their field and listen. This syncing up also helped my ability to communicate the frequency of correction to help restore proper function. It helps to understand how the body parts work as a team, but I couldn't ignore the other players of mind and spirit.

In my first 5 years of practice, I studied two tracks, structural and energetic. I spent 2 years in an advanced neurology program. The instructor taught the structural pathways of communication from the nervous system including the cellular level. It was very mechanical, no mention of the energies that animate the body. All of his solutions were how to identify dysfunctional neurology pathways and correct them.

The deeper I followed him down this rabbit hole, I knew a big something was missing.

The final straw was when we finally reached the long-awaited module that explained pain. I expected he would teach us the definitive pathways. He spent two days showing us paintings that depicted people in pain. He explained that pain is perceived in the brain. Perceived! Yes, there are pathways, but pain is something beyond pathways - it is in the emotional realm. That ended my pursuit for answers in his neurology model.

The energetic track taught me how to communicate with the body. It opened me to experiment with syncing up with my patient's energy field so I could listen more deeply. I found that the energetic field around the body strongly influences function of the body.

I searched to understand the phenomenon I was experiencing. I had learned to shift my awareness to access the subconscious communication highway of my patients. I had also learned how to communicate with energy beings who lent a guiding hand to help my patients, family, and friends.

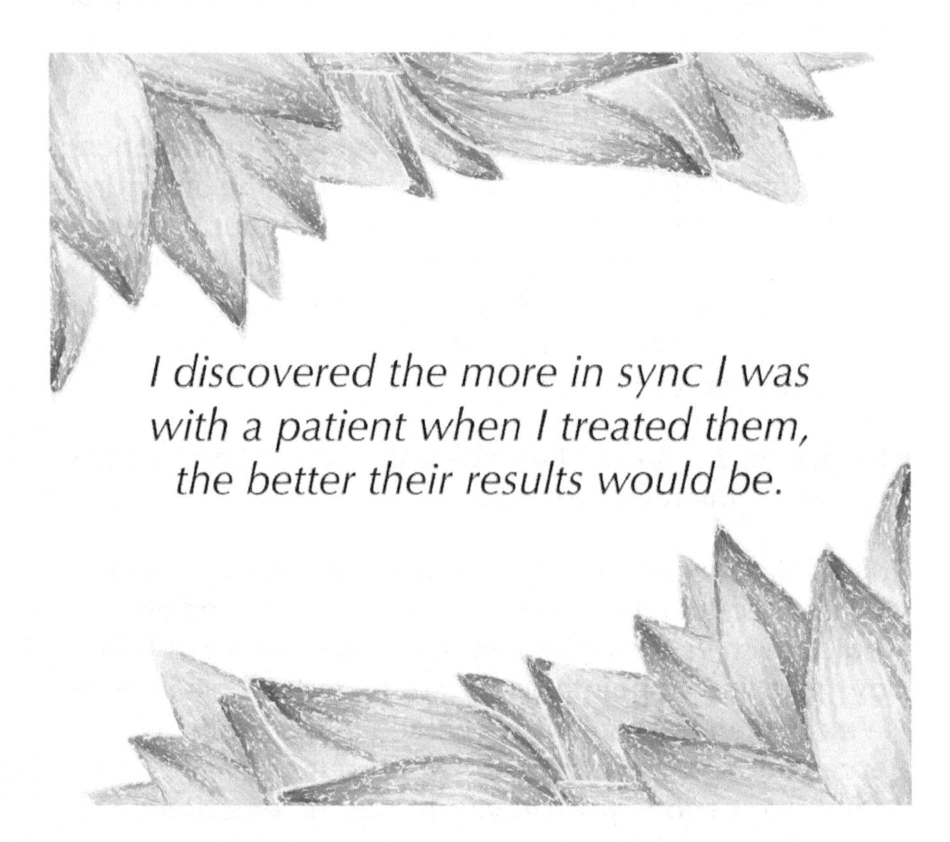

They say when the student is ready, the teacher appears. The ultimate guide revealed himself to me in Hawaii when Ram Dass touched my head and changed my world forever. That man in the blue blanket had decided it was time for me to become aware of his presence. It took seven more years before I met the team of Benevolent Beings who were waiting to assist me in the next leg of my Soul's journey.

The Jewels

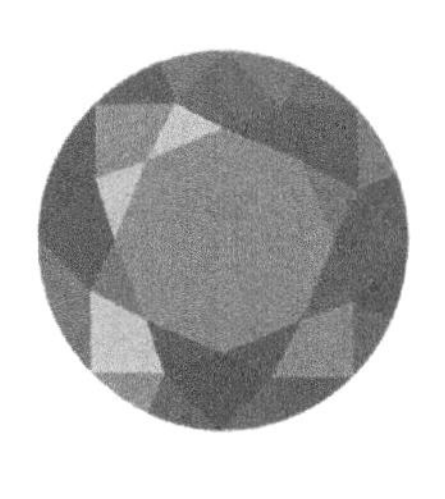

The first jewel is
100% light in
your tank.

Anything that
blocks your
connection to
the light is
preventing you
from accessing
your Soul's
Mastery.

1. Let your light shine

Everyone has a light within. Your light is encapsulated in an egg-shaped shell that emanates from your heart center. This shell is like your car's gas tank, it is the source of your Soul's fuel. This light is a beacon to all the Soul's around you. It is important to maintain this light and keep your shell intact.

You'd think that it is easy to keep that light going without any effort or having to pay attention to it, that it would be automatic.

You live in a world of duality: Good and Evil, Light and Dark, Good Guys and Bad Guys. The fastest way to derail and disempower a Soul in their life's mission is to separate it from its light source. Bad guys know how to poke holes in your light's protective shell. They can even knock out big chunks of your shell causing your light to spill out into your field. This weakens you.

One of my clients had been seeking answers in her metaphysical journey. She had gone to a variety of psychics, intuitives, and energetic healers trying to improve herself. She had been innocently seeking help. My Benevolent Beings (BBs) showed me that she had over 3,000 pinholes and 18 large holes that had caused almost half of her protective shell to be destroyed.

When you are influenced by the dark forces, the repeated immersion in the frequencies of the dark forces allow the dark forces to drill pin holes into your protective shell so the light leaks out into the field around you. Ultimately this drains you of your light. You become removed from your Soul's divinity and enslaved to the dark forces. The dark forces become like a tractor beam that corrupts your possibility, disabling you.

It is possible to restore the protective shell. My BBs explained there is a judicial court that oversees and rules on these situations. I was directed on how to present her case to this court. This court ruled that every dark force entity that was responsible for the damage to her shell had violated her free will by pretending to help her when in fact they were harming her. The court restored her protective shell. Now her Soul has its light energy source restored.

There is an aperture at the top of the protective shell that is a connection to the light to refill. Some people give their light away through that aperture for causes they think are worthy. Another of my clients was giving away almost 30% of her light to help a family member. Once I told her about it, she made a conscious choice to stop giving her light away and with the help of my BBs her tank was refilled and the aperture closed.

The first jewel in the Soul Mastery Journey is 100% light in your tank. The most important part of your mastery foundation is to be fully fueled on your journey. Anything that blocks your connection to the light is preventing you from accessing your Soul's Mastery.

The second jewel is being in alignment with Your Truth.
Your Truth is your homing beacon. It is your North Star, guiding you forward as you fulfill your Soul's mission.

2. Truth or Consequences

Your Truth is like the North Star, guiding you in your life choices to support your Soul's mission. Unfortunately, it is way too easy to get off track and separated from your truth. There are so many distorted thought forms and corrupted beliefs surrounding you, it is challenging for you to stay in alignment with your truth. There is a saying "Truth will set you free." This is very true when it comes to the way Your Truth will free you from all of the distractions and detours along your journey to fulfill your destiny.

The shortest distance between two points is a straight line. Your Truth is like a homing beacon that keeps reminding you of what you are here to do and who you really are. The consequences of being misdirected can pull you way off course and cause you to feel hopeless and wandering aimlessly, never seeming to be able to feel like you are making the difference you came here to make.

Being in alignment with Your Truth makes it easier to hear your Soul whispering instructions on how to achieve your journey.

When I was 29, I went to a Chiropractor for the first time. When I was 6 years old, I was in a car accident where I was catapulted from the back seat and hit the top of my head on the windshield. I can still vividly see that circular fracture in the glass with my blonde hairs stuck in it.

The resulting neck injury was never treated. My neck really didn't hurt, but I couldn't turn my head more than

45 degrees in either direction. I should have been able to turn twice as far.

There was something magical about receiving those Chiropractic adjustments. It inspired me to want to do that for other people. At first it was a whisper that grew louder. There was something deep within me that compelled me to find out what the academic requirements were. I squeezed in the classes and fulfilled every requirement while I worked full time.

Those pre admittance courses were challenging. I was struggling in my physics class. I went to my professor one morning and told him I thought I was going to have a nervous breakdown. His reply was I was the second one that morning! He made me laugh and he told me I'd be OK, not to worry. He was right. I made it through organic chemistry too.

Looking back, everything was in alignment for me to become a Chiropractor. I was even offered a buyout from my job in TV, which helped fund part of my tuition and living expenses too. Some would say I was in the right place at the right time. I say everything worked perfectly because I was in alignment with what I came here to do.

When I announced my intention to go to Chiropractic College, one of my coworkers told me that he too had considered becoming a Chiropractor. He said that he did the math and decided that he would not be able to support his family if he did that, so he gave up on that dream. Several years later, while I was in Chiropractic College, he died in a car accident. It made me very sad.

Part of me wondered - was that because he didn't follow his dream?

I knew that come hell or high water, I was going to do whatever it took to follow my dream to become a Chiropractor, and I did.

The second jewel in your Soul Mastery Journey is being in alignment with Your Truth. Your Truth is your homing beacon - it keeps reminding you of who you really are and what you are here to do. It is your North Star, guiding you forward as you fulfill your Soul's mission.

The third jewel identifies and removes the obstacles distorting your light body's alignment and function, so you can step fully into your Soul's Mastery.

3. You Light Up My Life

Everyone has a holographic light body. It is nourished by the Light of the Creator. The same light that fills your tank and fuels your connection with your Soul. Your ability to fully receive this light can be compromised by unfortunate, negative experiences that act like a black out curtain that separates you from it. Situations where you became convinced of your inability to overcome challenging situations and defined yourself accordingly. These self-beliefs separated you from your potential and became obstacles to access your Soul's Mastery.

If you, like other of my clients, were born into abusive family situations, you surely did the best you could under the circumstances. You most likely used every resource you had to navigate the disfunction. Unfortunately, along the way you may have embraced some limiting beliefs that became blackout curtains separating you from the Light.

Here are some examples:

- *Everyone's intuition is better than mine.*
- *I am destined to be all alone.*
- *Rejection is my ultimate punishment.*
- *In order to be free I have to allow society to persecute me.*
- *I'm ashamed to admit my gifts and talents.*
- *I have to work like an ant to fulfill my destiny.*
- *If I don't shoulder people's burdens, I will be all alone.*
- *The world is a very unfriendly place, I must hide to protect myself.*
- *My destiny is to be abandoned by the light*

because of the sins of my father.

- *Abuse is unavoidable; therefore, I must be careful to not anger my abusers by resisting. I must comply with or hide from my abusers.*
- *The Earth is a torture chamber.*
- *Loss is my companion; therefore, I must embrace this as a condition of my existence.*
- *Uncertainty at death.*
- *I can't accept my higher abilities*
- *Suffering is unavoidable.*
- *Life can't be easy.*
- *Cancer can eat me alive.*
- *Parasites are unavoidable so I have to coexist with them.*
- *My intuition is smaller than others.*

Clearly these types of deep-seated, limiting beliefs can be roadblocks to your pursuit of your life's purpose.

The clients who've had these types of beliefs dissolved away have found a new sense of freedom and purpose. They have found peace where there was conflict, strength where there was weakness and hope where there was hopelessness. They say they feel more inspired and confident. They all have felt more connected to their life's purpose and their Soul's mission.

Now is your opportunity to pull back the curtains blocking the Light that supports your Soul's mission.

The third jewel along your Soul Mastery Journey identifies and removes the roadblocks and obstacles distorting your holographic light body's proper alignment and function. When the distortion is removed, you are entirely prepared to step fully into your Soul's Mastery.

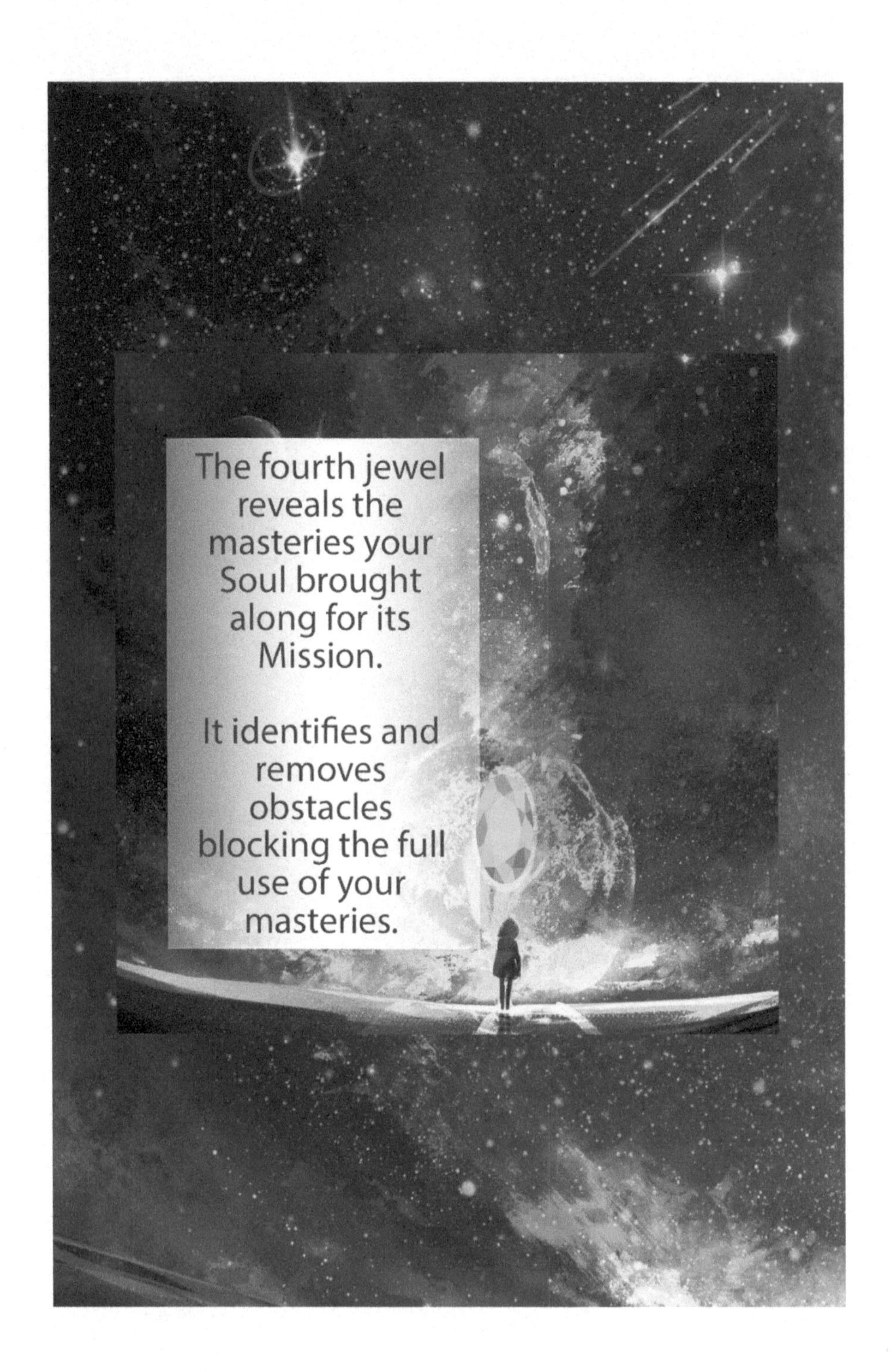
The fourth jewel reveals the masteries your Soul brought along for its Mission.
It identifies and removes obstacles blocking the full use of your masteries.

4. Lost and Found

Actors improve their craft with every new project that stretches them to grow. Each new role gives them an opportunity to expand their performance skillset library. The same goes for your Soul. Each incarnation gives it a new role to play. Your Soul can use skills it already mastered or master some new ones.

I was quite surprised when my BBs introduced this concept to me. I was asking for clarification on what my Soul came here to do. Who could I help and how? I had never heard about Soul's acquiring Mastery with each mission. It makes sense that they could. I believed I came into this body with a specific mission. I was determined to figure out how to accomplish it.

Gradually my BBs started to reveal bits and pieces of my Soul's Mastery. While my personality is in complete awe of my Soul's accomplishments, the BBs know what I'm capable of and are patiently showing me the way.

I was working with a client to clear her curtains of separation. She had a huge block that was coming from another dimension. I asked my highest-level BBs how to remove it? They explained it was origination in another dimension and they would take me there to negotiate its removal.

When we arrived in that dimension, I saw a large, towering building. Strangely, it felt like Harry Potter. The sensation was so strong that I couldn't help but wonder if this place was where JK Rowling drew her inspiration. We went into a very large room with a very high ceiling. A council was already assembled to meet with us.

They explained that the big block was because my client pledged her undying love to a guy whose family line was cursed. If she were to withdraw this pledge, they would remove the block.

I thanked them for being willing to help my client.

They said, before you leave, we want to ask you a personal question. They showed me an energetic thought form - it looked like a ball of energy. I listened to it and what came to mind was a very difficult situation from a different lifetime.

I told them that situation was a really hard time for me. I made some great personal sacrifices and it took a huge toll on me. They then revealed how in that lifetime I took out the best Sorcerer they ever had. WOW! That explained why I had the impression the place was like Harry Potter when I arrived.

I was stunned by their news. I apologized for having to do that and I wish we could all live in peace. I told them about the extremely loving Benevolent Beings I have recently met and how I wished we could all be like them.

Once I returned back home, I couldn't help thinking about it. I showed up to their council armed with very high-level BBs. They recognized me from before. They understood the level of mastery I had achieved. They could see that in this current lifetime I had the ability to travel to their dimension and make a request. They didn't attack me: was it out of respect or out of fear?

They did honor their word. My client withdrew her pledge of undying love and they removed the big blockage in her field.

Some Souls incarnate to gain mastery. One of my client's Soul Mission is to achieve self-expression mastery. She had blocks around using her voice and having to please authority figures, because it could threaten her survival if she did. She could absolutely relate to both of those struggles. Even her human design chart shows authority to be a huge shadow for her to have to deal with.

She told me that she could see situations all through her life how she was wired and conditioned to respect and follow experts/authorities. To compensate, she became an overachiever in college as valedictorian in her Ivy League school to prove her worth. However, she is the only divorced person in her extended family, the only one without a 'real job' as an online successful entrepreneur.

She said "I had somehow broken away on the outside, but on the inside, there was still that little girl who needed to get the A+. It was like, if I just tuck myself under the aegis of some authority, I'll be safe, successful, and loved." In business she aligned with male experts because she was afraid to challenge the patriarchal model. After her corrective treatments she said "Things now feel more aligned, like my tank has an endless supply of high-octane fuel. I am woman hear me roar and f you if you don't like it lol."

Below are some examples of the Soul Mastery achievements that some of my clients brought in to achieve their Soul Mission.

Take someone's spark and make it a flame. She can ignite people's inner calling.

Relinquish connections, like weeding a garden, to nurture and aid emerging connections that matter to a

Soul's mission.

Rejection of limitation barriers to a Soul's advancement. (The ability to remove specific barriers to a Soul's advancement)

Ability to transversely travel through the dimensions influencing a person's connections with the light. This allows her to reestablish broken connections.

The ability to slip between dimensions to gain perspective on situations on how best to address them in order to orchestrate solutions with the least amount of effort.

The ability to shift her vibrational frequency to match the one's she helps, so they can resonate with that new frequency more efficiently to achieve their results faster.

By being a beacon of light, she attracts the people she is here to guide with her ability to resonate with them.

Ability to instill hope. (This is a very high-level mastery)

There are 4 energetic entry points that exist in the mental body of every organism. She has the ability to access these 4 entry points to influence spiritual advancement.

The power of connection. She is able to connect to 7 dimensions.

Her intuition spans 2 portals that are the conduits for direct response to her questions.

Listening to the potential that exists in the possible futures that are aligned with an individual

She weaves destiny, opportunity, desperation, unwavering allegiance, and fierce self-reformation.

Ability to shift into resonance with others to form rapport that allows her to match their wavelength to transcend resistance to remembering who they are.

Ability to take a stand. Unwavering in his principles because he can take a stand. He can lift people up to have confidence in their own missions.

Resourcefulness

Infectious happiness

After treating the energetic roadblocks and obstacles to their Soul Mastery, they are able to access and use these tools in their daily life as needed.

Since you are reading this book, there is a very good chance that you have equally powerful Soul Mastery Skillset of talents and tools. You too may have some obstacles to overcome in order to use them.

The fourth jewel in your Soul Mastery Journey has three parts. First it reveals the masteries your Soul chose to bring along to accomplish its Mission. Next, it identifies the obstacles blocking your use of your masteries. Finally, these obstacles are removed so you regain full access to them.

The fifth jewel
connects you
with your
Spiritual Lineage.

Your Spiritual
Ancestors
powerfully and
gently guide you
in the journey of
your Soul's
Mission.

5. Blessings

Things that happen randomly and naturally seem to come out of nowhere. What if everything that has ever happened to you was a form of a blessing? Looking back at my life, I can see that now. I certainly didn't recognize that then. Oftentimes situations would overwhelm me and make me feel sad or make me feel like I wasn't in control or that I was a victim or that God really didn't love me after all.

- Have you felt that way too?
- Like why would this bad thing happen to me?
- Why would it be so hard to dig out of the hole I'm in?
- What's my life purpose?
- Why am I here?
- What's the meaning of life?

So many unanswered questions. Yet living in the moment one could realize that every moment is a blessing and every piece of the puzzle goes together eventually.

One of your greatest blessings is your spiritual lineage. Your spiritual lineage is a team specific to you. It is there to blow like the wind through your hair to help guide you gently along in your journey of your Soul's mission. Your spiritual lineage is all around you and is looking out for you. The better the connection you have to your spiritual lineage, the more aware of your blessings you will become.

I was born into a family that believed in Jesus and went to church when I was a kid. I had the opportunity to go to a private Lutheran school from kindergarten to sixth grade. I had the opportunity to go to Sunday school and learn Bible stories that told me Jesus loved me. There was a Father, Son, and Holy Ghost. I never really understood the white bird. But I knew it was important. I had a strong affinity for trusting and believing this story about Jesus and God in the Bible. My church was very neutral and non-judgmental, they weren't hellfire and brimstone. There was a gentle kindness to their Jesus who died for my sins.

Their God the Father was loving and kind. He could be judgmental, but for the most part, he was there to be like a good grandpa to me. God had a special kind of feeling for me. I heard a poem that the local TV station announcer would read every night before the station signed off. I watched it once, then I was hooked. I'd stay up late just so I could hear this poem again.

A World War II pilot wrote a poem called High Flight. The words were so vivid I felt like I was in the plane with him. I could feel the movements. I could see what he was seeing. It was so exciting to break free of the earth and soar. Somehow by being in that plane, I had broken the chains that kept me on earth, separated from God.

"High Flight" by John G. Magee on September 3, 1941

Oh! I have slipped the surly bonds of Earth
And danced the skies on laughter-silvered wings;
Sunward I've climbed, and joined the tumbling mirth
of sun-split clouds,-and done a hundred things
You have not dreamed of-wheeled and soared and swung
High in the sunlit silence. Hov'ring there,
I've chased the shouting wind along, and flung
My eager craft through footless halls of air....
Up, up the long, delirious, burning blue
I've topped the wind-swept heights with easy grace
Where never lark nor ever eagle flew-
And, while with silent lifting mind I've trod
The high untrespassed sanctity of space,
Put out my hand, and touched the face of God

(https://www.nationalmuseum.af.mil/Visit/Museum-Exhibits/Fact-Sheets/Display/Article/196844/pilot-officer-john-gillespie-magee-high-flight/)

I could feel myself reaching out and touching the face of God. There was something so true about that to me. It was such a important impression that I would wake up at night just in time to go into the living room and turn on the TV and wait for them to read it. I wanted to hear it one more time. It meant so much to me, because it was so real to me. What I didn't realize is that this was my way of remembering who I am. Remembering my connection to my God, my Creator thanks to my lineage who amplified the signal of the Creator to remind me who I am and why I'm here.

Your lineage whispers to you in ways that are specific to you. It could be nature, music, or whatever it may be, that you are so lost in the beauty around you that your lineage can remind you who you are.

Seeing your world through the eyes of "everything is a blessing" does have the power to see things very differently. What if all the hurts or situations where you feel disempowered were how the Creator moves and expresses through you?

What if every situation actually benefits you, whether it's a win or a loss?

What if it is an opportunity to love the ones who harm you?

What if it is an opportunity to hold your head up high and move forward with grace?

What if it is an opportunity to overcome and learn how to be resilient?

One of the greatest abilities is resilience. To be resilient and pick yourself up when you get knocked down. To have a reason that's bigger than yourself. One that gets you up in the morning and keeps you going on those really long, hard stretches.

Once you know that you have a Spiritual lineage surrounding you, assisting and guiding you - you'll know that you're never alone.

You actually are never ever alone.

You have never been alone.

You will never be alone.

It just feels that way until you realize you have an invisible team. Some blessings require a major shift in perspective. Finding a way to redefine your life experiences with the people who victimized and hurt you. To step outside the experience and view it like a movie where you are an actor who played a painful role that somehow benefited you. Somehow, it's a blessing to you. Perhaps death taking a loved one who you deeply miss, or the loss of job or career.

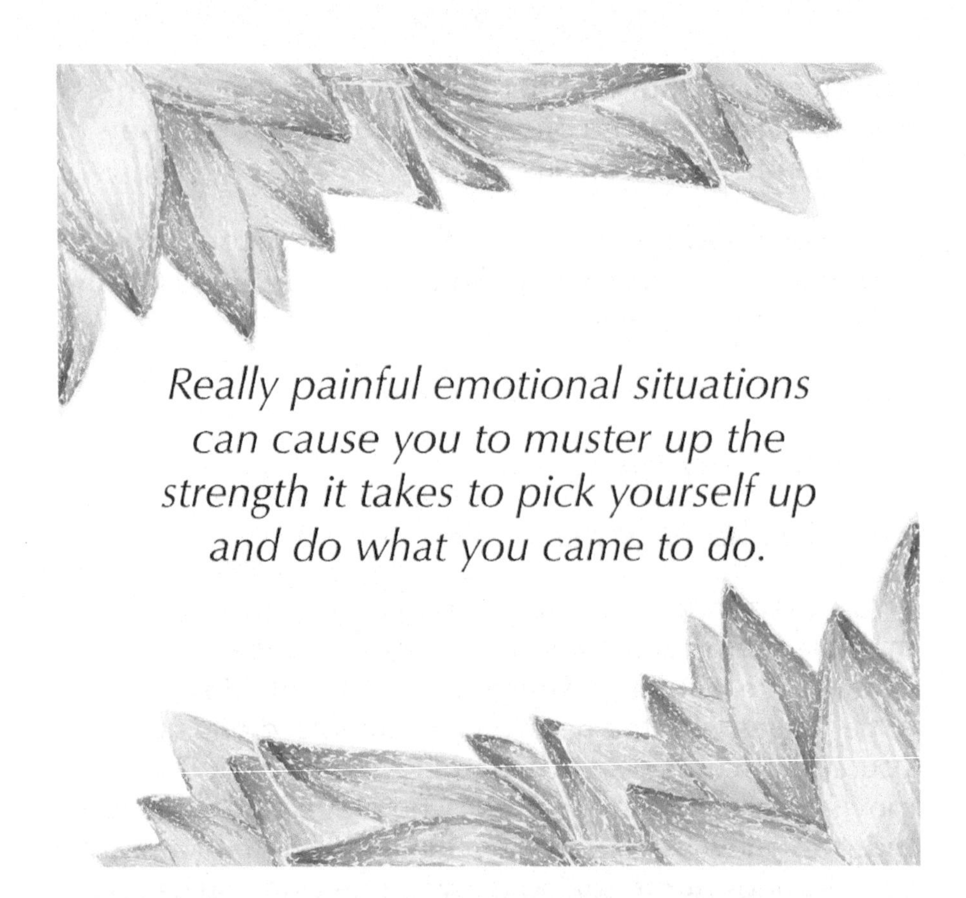

What if you could face every adversity with the conviction of knowing that you have the support of an unseen team with the perspective that everything is a blessing? Perspective is everything. Your harsh self-judgment isn't your friend. Judgment can make you a prisoner chained to the outrageous conclusions your mind came up with.

Breaking free of these judgments and stories is the result of your resilience and ability to have a perspective that everything is a blessing.

Being saddled with heavy burdens doesn't seem like a blessing at all. These upsetting, real-life burdens seem like punishments. It could feel like another punishment when someone dares to suggest that everything is a blessing. You live in a world that is full of obstacles and challenges, as well as synchronicity and opportunities.

Opportunities to overcome, opportunities to be grateful, opportunities to see the world through other people's eyes who have a different view. Your peace and freedom depend on your ability to step back and be an observer, rather than identify as a prisoner. You may never know the reason for it in this lifetime.

You have a choice of being super grateful or super resentful. Which vibration do you prefer to be? The experience is happening any way. So many people have overcome adversity purely through their perspective of that adversity. Something inside them woke up and wouldn't allow themselves to be broken by their captors or oppressors. Somehow, they were able to see past the negative to see the positive. You have the opportunity to see blessings everywhere you look.

The fifth jewel of your Soul Mastery Journey connects you with your Spiritual Lineage. Your Spiritual Ancestors powerfully and gently guide you in the journey of your Soul's Mission. Take heart that they are influencing and supporting you with blessings every step of the way.

The sixth jewel activates your Spiritual Sovereignty.
This awakening empowerment supports your Soul's Mission to lead people out of Spiritual Prison.

6. If I Only Knew

If I only knew that when I came into this world... what an adventure awaited me! Before I slipped into the envelope of Earth, I understood much greater things. I understood that the reason I was joining this mission was because the Earth had achieved a place of advancement that it was ready for operatives like me.

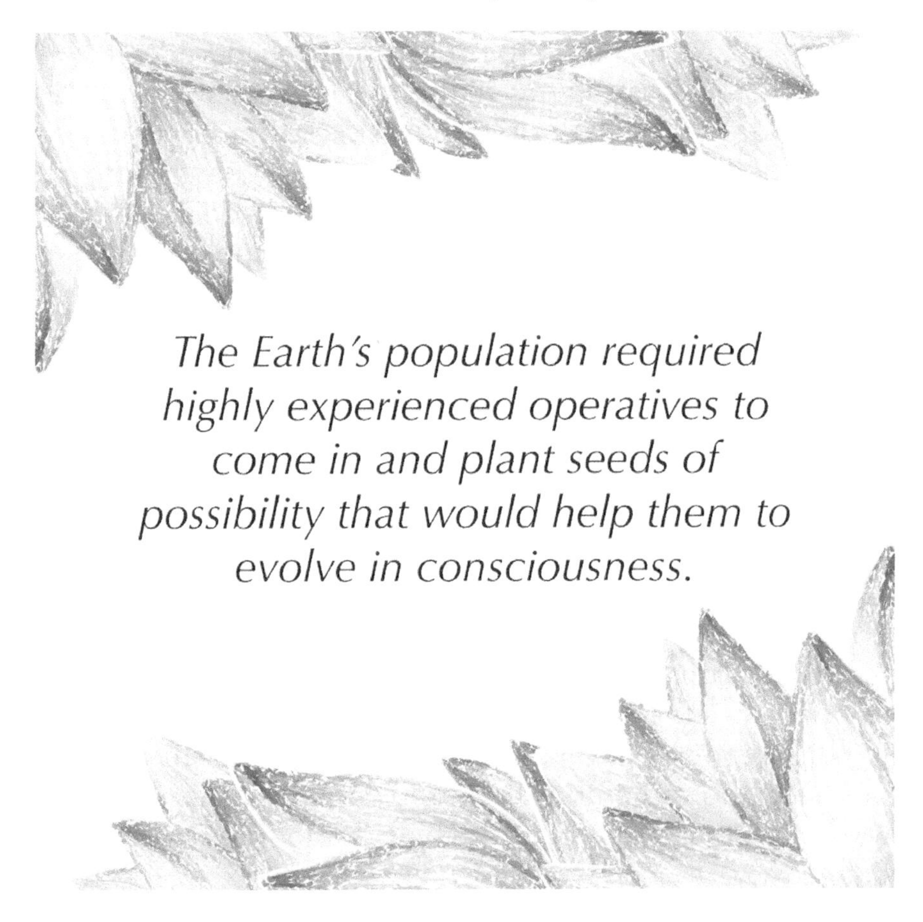

The Earth's population required highly experienced operatives to come in and plant seeds of possibility that would help them to evolve in consciousness.

Armies of operatives have come in waves, to help advance the consciousness on this little blue planet. I knew that I might not be able to remember who I was and why I was here. Since I had overcome that in so many operations, I felt confident that I would be able to remember in this time as well.

The most valuable asset I had going for me was my Spiritual Sovereignty. I had achieved Sovereignty many missions ago and have been successful in maintaining it in all of my missions since then.

As an awake, alert, productive operative, my team of Benevolent Beings and Spiritual Lineage worked with me on a daily basis in my childhood. My every move was orchestrated with their guidance. No matter how easy or how difficult a day, every situation was orchestrated. Every experience and interaction was very deliberate. These experiences were there to sharpen the blade to prepare me for what laid ahead.

I interacted with other operatives who were here on the same important mission. As we crossed paths, our energy fields touched each other. We experienced a huge remembering between us similar to how, in the forest, the tree's roots communicate to one another. We operatives, who were here on this mission of awakening, remind each other why we are here.

Some operatives have fallen into darkness and can't remember. The rest of us have done everything we can to help them to remember and to awaken to why they are here and remember their Soul Mastery. This body of work, the Soul Mastery Journey, is to do that in a very public way.

It's important that the operatives like you, who are here to make a difference, remember who they are. If this body of work speaks to you, you most likely are a part of this army. It will remind you that you are here with a special mission. You will feel the need to remember who you are and gain access to the mastery tools you brought with you or acquire the tools that you are here to gain and master.

Not everyone who incarnates on Earth is here to use their mastery or to gain mastery. Not everyone has an internal urging of important destiny. They're here to learn, experience and add to the collective. They aren't here to lead the collective. The people who need to know about their mastery are the leaders. They have come to raise awareness in consciousness, so the little blue planet can move towards unity and away from duality. To move towards love, instead of the division of good and evil.

There are much greater degrees of love and understanding of love to be achieved and experienced. The Creator's love expresses a bliss so extreme that human beings actually can't handle it. Your Soul has experienced this. You have come to join with this army to raise consciousness on Earth.

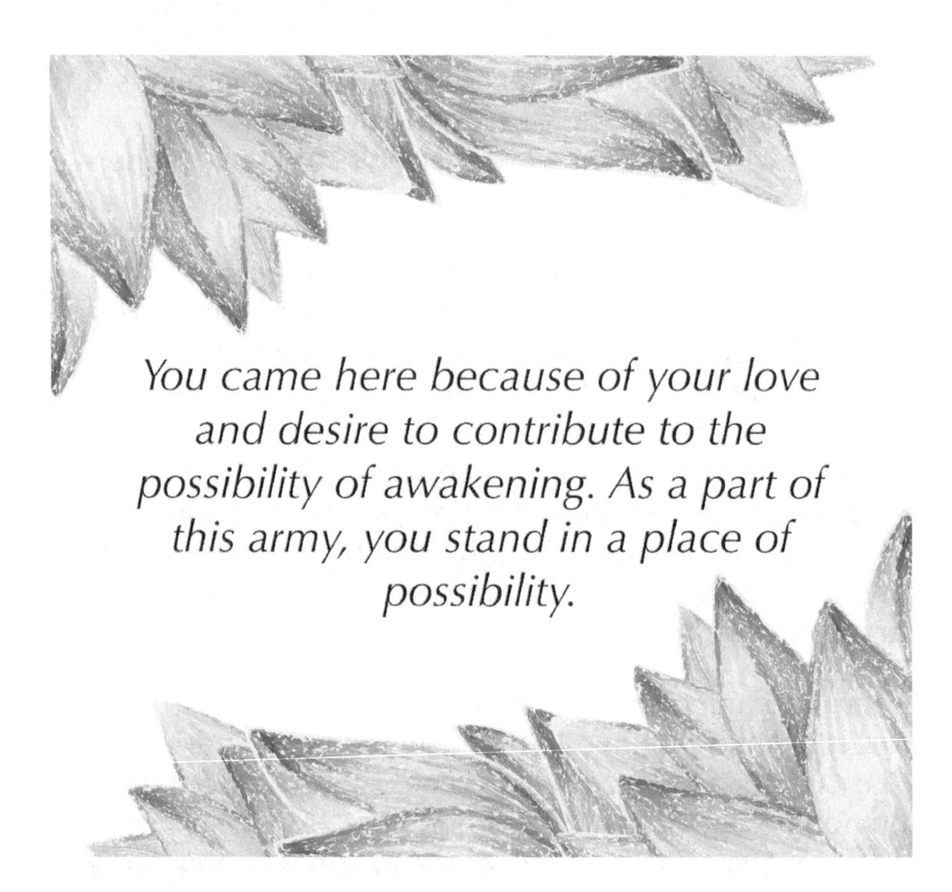

There are no guarantees, yet you came just the same. Success is better achieved by the awakening, and remembering who you are and why you're here.

Understand that there truly are agents who are very deliberate in their attempts to prevent this awakening. These agents have acquired great skills that should be deeply respected. Your army is not here to have a battle. You've done that before. And you have paid the price of those battles. You're not here to start a war.

Society and its cultures have throttled humanity's expression of possibility. Mankind's greed and its belief of "there isn't enough" has led to very destructive behaviors. It has been a very difficult long battle to awaken and raise consciousness. The good news is extraordinary, advanced Benevolent Beings have come in the name of love to lead humans out of the darkness by helping them to awaken to their truth and succeed in their Soul's mission.

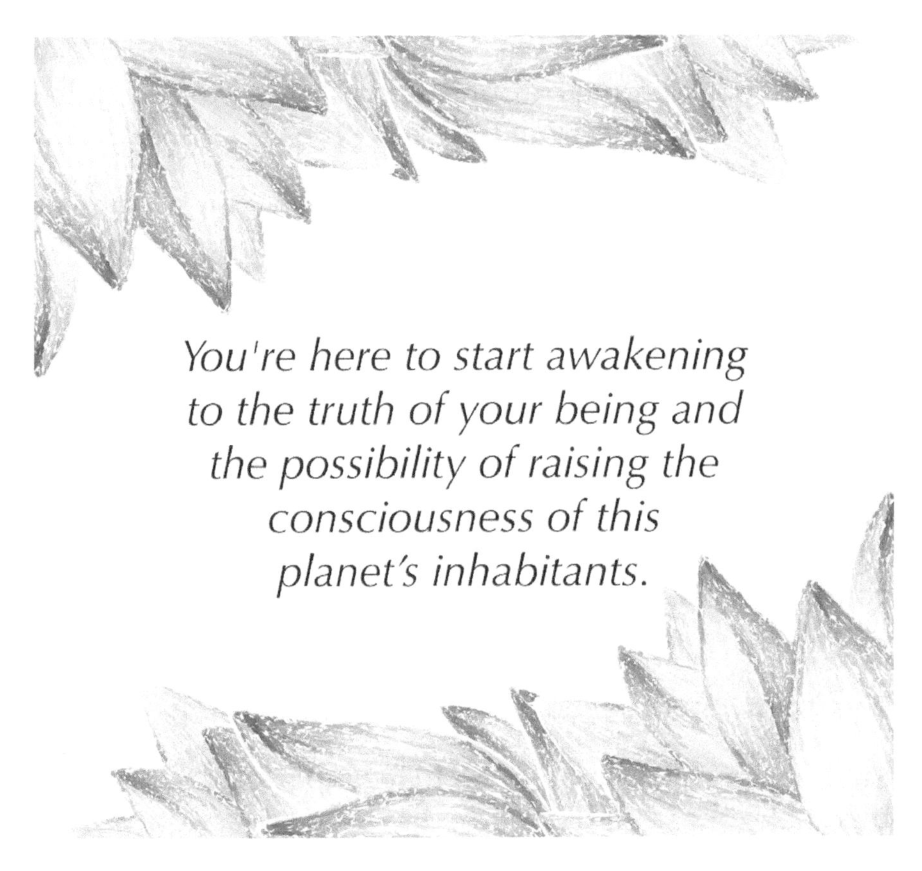

The overly simplified stories of good and evil, of Satan and God, depict that struggle and dichotomy. Waking up inside the dream within the construct of duality is the challenge you and your fellow armies face.

As an operative, you have come to promote enlightenment, expand Spiritual awareness, and express the possibility of how love can expand to even greater and greater lengths. You're here to awaken and listen to the voice of your Soul so you can do what you came to do.

You are here to add sweetness and help shift consciousness to overcome the lower vibrations of greed, war, tyranny and oppression.

What do people gain by oppressing? What do they gain by stealing the light from others?

This behavior keeps humanity in a prison. You bring the opportunity to lead people out of this Spiritual prison. Once you experience the magnitude of love that the Benevolent Beings have for you, it will help you to awaken and step into your Spiritual mastery.

You will join the army to raise consciousness on this planet as you bring forth your Soul's message. Your army will influence the consciousness of the solar systems that interact with Earth and especially the consciousness of the evil ones who are deliberately undermining love, integrity, honesty.

This is why Spiritual Sovereignty is so important.

Sovereignty allows you to be fully empowered. You may be among those who already achieved sovereignty but are separated from it. The purpose of this work is to empower you and the army of light that has incarnated at this opportune time.

The Soul Mastery Journey reveals important information about you. Your personal analysis uncovers the Mastery Skillset your Soul brought in for this mission and if there are any energetic blockages preventing you from using these skills.

Once these masteries are restored, the most powerful tool you can ever have in your toolbox is to be fully connected to your Spiritual Lineage and activated with them to achieve your Spiritual Sovereignty.

Destiny

Destiny is an interesting concept. Some think they are in the driver's seat when it comes to their destiny, while others feel like they're being dragged through broken glass.

Every story has an arc of the beginning, middle, and end. Is destiny the beginning? The middle? The end? Could it be that destiny is the whole story? Your world is filled with so many interactions and possibilities of outcomes. It's a magical dance. Who are you going to dance with today and how will you choose to dance with them?

What is your dance? Where will you dance? Why will you dance? Does it matter? Destiny... What is your destiny in every second of the day of your life?

Destiny is happening in the moment or is there some distant plan for the end? Is it what you achieve along the way or what you have to do in order to fulfill that conclusion? It certainly is an interesting perspective: destiny. When you think about it, you have a choice. You really do. Even if you feel like you don't.

You really do have a choice.

You have a choice to accept the dogma, the stories, the "shoulds," the judgments of society, of your family, of your God, of your teachers, of your authorities. Who is the authority? Are you the authority? Is everybody else the authority? Who's in charge? Mastery assumes there's a destiny. Mastery assumes that the Skillset that you have mastered are the tools that will help you to achieve the destiny that awaits you.

Mastery Skills are the gifts that you bring with you into this life. When your Soul makes the decision to incarnate in a physical body it chooses a specific physical body that it knows ahead of time will have various challenges and various opportunities. It understands the pluses and minuses. Regardless, your mastery tools will guide you and assist you to use the vehicle (body) you have chosen as you face the opportunities or struggles in this incarnation.

Astrology's influence is really interesting. The time and place that you're born has such a strong influence on your experience here. Astrology can tell you qualities about yourself that are pretty mind blowing sometimes. Like wow, I really do have those qualities. Your Soul chose your body and the timing. It chose your family situation and opportunities it offers. Your Soul came prepared.

Your destiny is actually every day, it isn't a finish line. Like every day. You make progress. It may seem that you travel a road that climbs up the mountain, down the mountain, around the mountain, and even through it. All of the opportunities to learn and to contribute. Contribution happens daily.

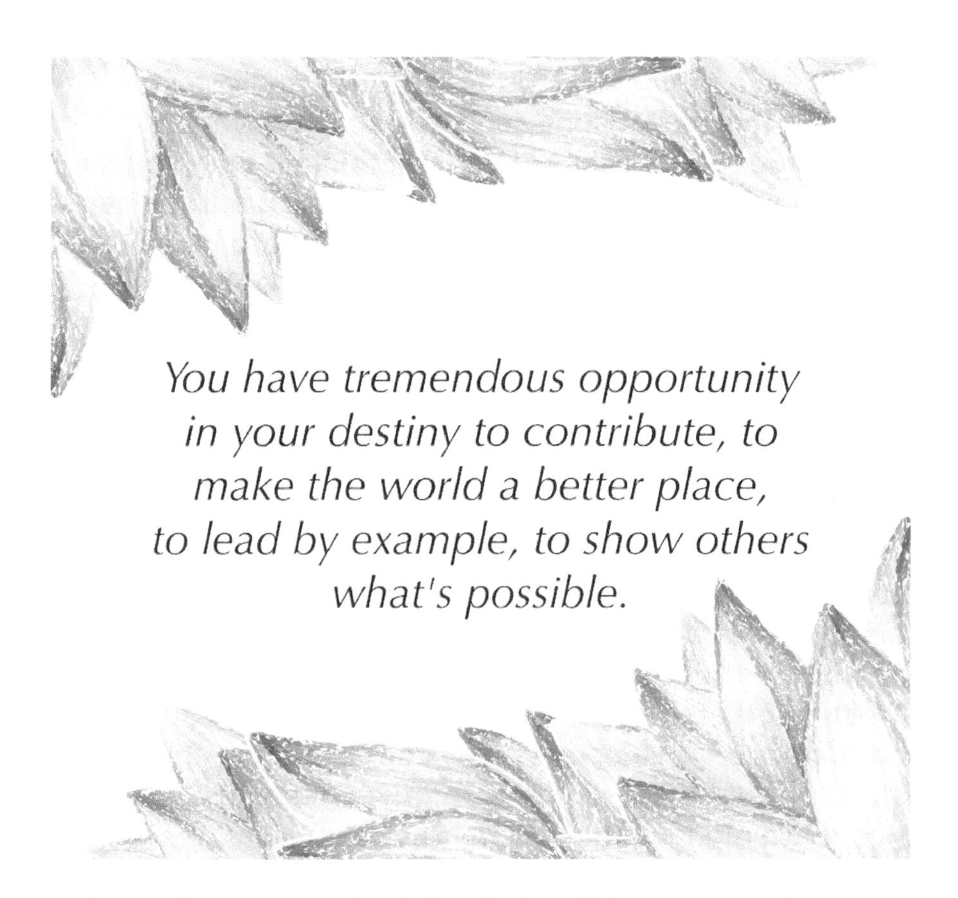

This reminds me of the joke. "Why did the armadillo cross the road? To prove to the chicken that it could be done." If you grew up in Texas, you know that armadillos are very often killed on the road. If an Armadillo makes it across - it really had to hustle. Destiny. You have so much opportunity. Every day is a new adventure. Sometimes the role that you play takes you through storms, disasters, agony, pain, and suffering. In every one of these seeming defeats there's a victory. A victory of accomplishing your destiny.

In order for some to understand their destiny, they want it laid out like a road map. They want directions so they will know when to turn, or distance to travel before they take an exit. They want to have it all laid out and it easy to follow. In reality, it already has been orchestrated. Reading this book is one such example. It's your destiny. Today you read this chapter. Something in this chapter fulfills your destiny today. The nice thing about destiny is there's a new opportunity presenting itself to you. Step by step, you fulfill what you came here to do. Your life purpose, your Soul's purpose, your Soul's mission. Your lineages, your team's mission. Your contribution to your fellow man. Destiny. What a beautiful thing. What a beautiful opportunity. What a beautiful way to view every day.

They say that hindsight is 2020. Looking ahead, you can't always see the forest for the trees. Often, perspective isn't obvious until after you've arrived at a destination. Was that shortcut a great idea? A bad idea? Trusting others worked or maybe you wished you hadn't? Your perspective helps you to analyze the strategies that led you here and the ones that slowed you down along with everything else you learned along the way.

Having full access to your Soul's mastery gives you greater autonomy. Now you stand more completely in your power as you have reached your spiritual Sovereignty. The beauty of your achieving goes out into the world in an energetic way and teaches everyone your achievement is possible. One person figures it out. Then the next person figures it out.

One example in history is the telegraph. The idea for the telegraph happened simultaneously in the United States and over in Europe. The credit for inventing the telegraph falls to two sets of researchers: Sir William Cooke (1806-79) and Sir Charles Wheatstone (1802-75) in England, and Samuel Morse (1791-1872), Leonard Gale

(1800-83), and Alfred Vail (1807-59) in the U.S. Could it be destiny that explains those types of synchronicities where one person gets the idea and on the other side of the world, another person gets the same idea and they both bring that idea forward?

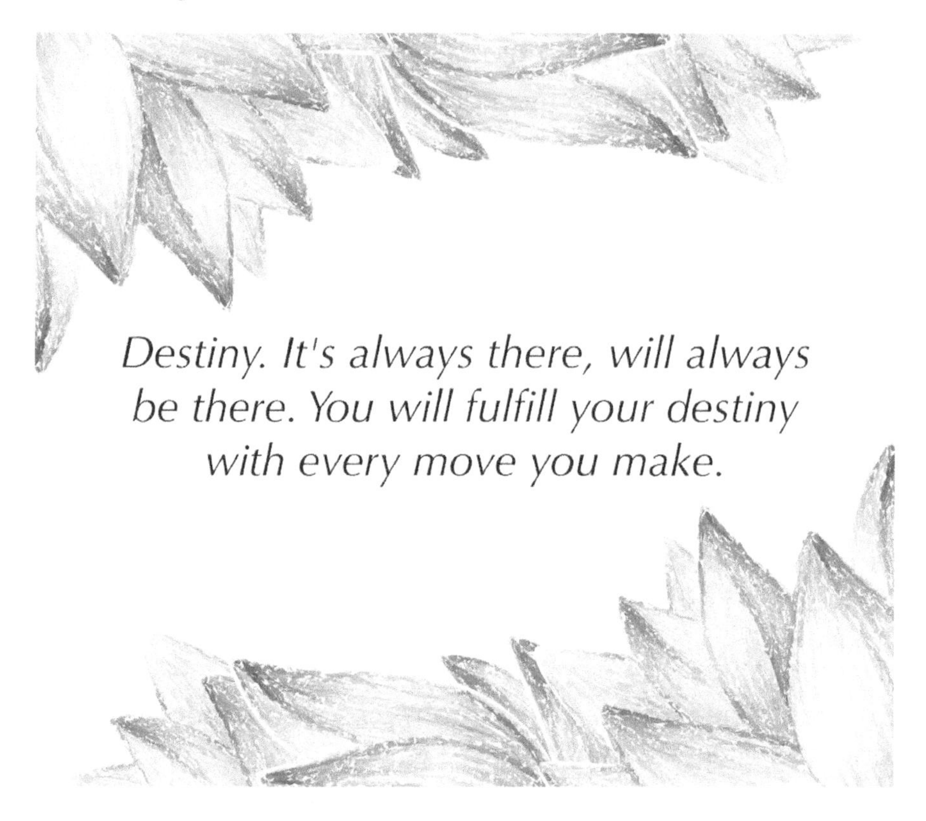

You have a toolkit of mastery that you achieved in your previous incarnations to assist you in your Soul's mission. You are a highly trained Soul-dier, much like a Navy Seal or a Green Beret, who inherently knows how to do what it takes to accomplish your Soul's mission. If you see yourself as a highly trained operative, your destiny seems so much easier. It's like a sure thing.

Every day you trust that these masteries you brought in with you are assisting you and helping you. You aren't alone, you have an energetic team. Your spiritual lineage connects you with your fellow Soul-diers who are in the same army as you. You are working with your team whether you're consciously aware of it or not.

Every little step adds up. The journey of 1,000 miles begins with one step. You're making a difference because you're achieving your Destiny every day.

Looking back over 5, 10, 20 years down the road gives you a lot more perspective of what you've achieved and what it took to get there. Your resilience, your perseverance, your determination along with your giftedness and your mastery that you brought in with you has made your journey easier, smoother, more effective.

Those who have been separated from their mastery, can totally relate to how difficult and challenging it's been. How it has taken everything they've got to get where they are. They know that there has to be more to the story.

In 1969, when I was 13, my mom played one song over and over. The Grammy Award winning song "Is that all there is." You can feel the deep dissatisfaction and longing in Peggy Lee's voice as she sings about how we might as well grab our moments of pleasure and enjoyment where we can find them because ultimately, life is nothing more than a meaningless series of disappointments. It left a deep impression on me; I never forgot it. Rather than feeling stuck and destined to an unhappy life, I longed for more. I just knew that there was more, a whole lot more, out there for me. You can probably relate as well.

That little voice whispering inside you, is urging you to

fulfill your destiny. The part of you who knows you have mastery talents and wants you to find them like hidden easter eggs.

That you have found this book and it speaks to you is because it's your destiny.

It's your destiny to learn more about yourself.

It's your destiny to step into your mastery to find out what your masteries are and to remove the blocks to your masteries, so you can step into the full power of your mastery.

It is your destiny to stand on the mountaintop. It is your destiny to achieve important things.

It is your destiny to help your fellow man.

It is your destiny to move mountains.

It is your destiny to raise the consciousness of humanity.

Your destiny is to experience Sovereignty, to have a deeper understanding of what you're capable of and to be connected with those capabilities. Congratulations on all of the perseverance and resilience that carried you up to today. Your time here is precious. Your contribution matters. Your Soul Mastery Journey is part of your destiny to fulfill your Soul's Mission with greater ease.

Autonomy

Standing on your own two feet reaching skyward, autonomy embraces you. You step firmly into your distinct and unique contribution. Once you have traveled your Soul Mastery Journey and achieved all six of the jewels, you are in a uniquely powerful position that supports you in your Soul's Mission. When you have discovered your Soul Mastery Skills, and all of the obstacles to utilize them have been removed, you are in the most powerful position that supports you in delivering the contribution you came to make.

Autonomy is the balancing act of how you will deal with all of the various situations you encounter. The power of standing in the bullseye of your mastery gives you the advantage you need in every situation. You become a lightning rod to receive all of the support, all of the opportunity, all of the synchronicity necessary to fulfill your Soul's mission.

Stepping into this power can, and often does, realign your world as you know it. You may encounter some detours. Unexpected detours that actually help you to experience opportunities you weren't able to connect with before.

It may seem like retrograde motion at times, as there are things that you have to go back and experience in order to have all that you need to succeed.

You will find that some people will leave your circle. You may feel some concern or upset, but know that it's important that they leave your circle in order for you to achieve your mission. You will find new support and new opportunities to use your mastery tools. Sometimes you'll find so many doors closing it will make you question if you made the right choice.

Looking back, when I read the email from my landlady saying she had made the difficult decision to sell the duplex I had been living in for almost 15 years, I was struck by a lightning bolt that made my heart race. I knew with the real estate market being as hot as it was that the place would sell within a week of listing and then I would have 60 days to get out. I was faced with having to pack up almost 30 years of my life in 60 days and find an affordable place to live. It was a terrifying new reality for me that shook my world.

April of 2018 was a horrible month for me. Not only did I find out I had to move, I also found out that my friend Richard was diagnosed with stage four colon cancer. I had no idea that this serious downsizing and move that I was forced to make in June actually prepared me for Richard's death five months later. Going back to the Chinese parable of the farmer and his horse...was it good or bad?

This serious downsizing made it much easier to make the move from California to Virginia in 2020.

Looking back, it all made perfect sense.

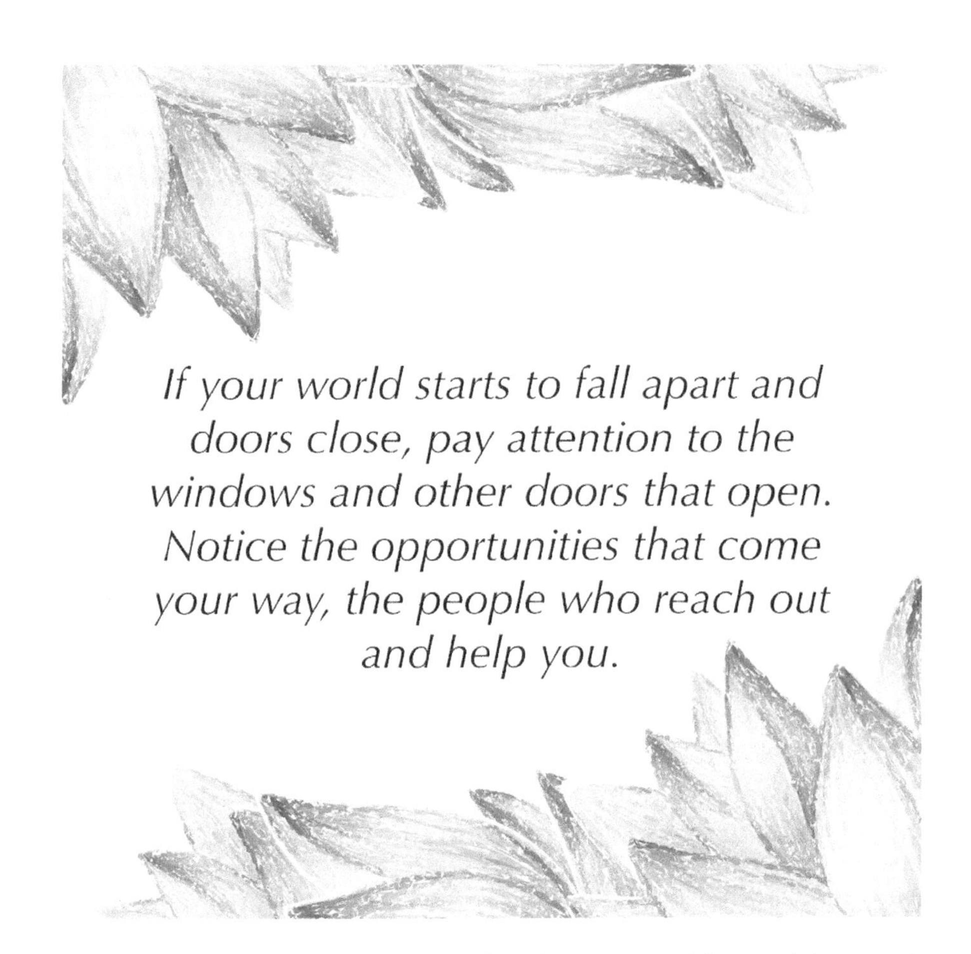

When my world fell apart, friends stepped in and formed that safety net that gave me a safe-haven while I weathered the storm of change that has allowed me to bring Soul Mastery Journey into reality.

You too will have similar experiences of doors opening and closing. I invite you to keep the faith and know that synchronicity is happening in your favor. Even if it looks like everything around you is crumbling and dying. There's absolutely new growth underneath it all.

I made the decision to become a Chiropractor when I was 29 years old. It took me almost three years to get my education prerequisites so I could go to chiropractic college. An interesting synchronicity was how my employer wanted to downsize and was offering buyouts just as I was ready to start Chiropractic school. I went to personnel and told them I was interested.

As luck would have it, the manager who could have declined my request didn't attend the meeting where my name was discussed. The company offered me a buyout much to my managers disappointment. The synchronicity of my manager missing that meeting intersected with my planning to leave anyway. I was given a buyout opportunity that helped to bridge and pay for part of that transition to start my new career.

It took 35 more years before I could see how all the pieces fell so easily into place, dovetailing with my Soul's Mastery expressing. Looking back, I can see where my Soul Mastery actually kicked in and acted as a lightning rod hitting the bullseye for all of the synchronistic events that were necessary for me to achieve my Soul's Mission.

You are ahead of the game as you step into your Autonomy when you are able to fully access your Soul Mastery tools. You will have insights and start to understand how the pieces of your life experience puzzle came together. You have a supreme advantage of having the confidence of knowing that it's all working out. There's a synchronistic plan unfolding as you step into the fast lane of achieving your Soul's Mission.

Stepping into your bullseye of Mastery catapults you to achieve greater things. You will move forward in a way that best serves your destiny. You will be connected with your lineage and it will be fully activated, which means everything that happens is for your benefit. You will have the opportunity to have the perspective of understanding that no matter how unpleasant a situation, you will understand that this situation is pushing you further along in succeeding in your Mission.

Keep the faith even in the thunderstorms as much as on a sunny day. Keep the faith in knowing that your Soul Mastery Skills are helping you, guiding and empowering you to achieve your Soul's Mission.

Your Invitation...

Are you ready to discover your Soul Mastery Skillset, and if there's anything preventing you from fully using your skills, talents, and tools you were born with when you came into this body?

Head over to **www.SoulMasteryJourney.com** to start your Soul Mastery Journey.

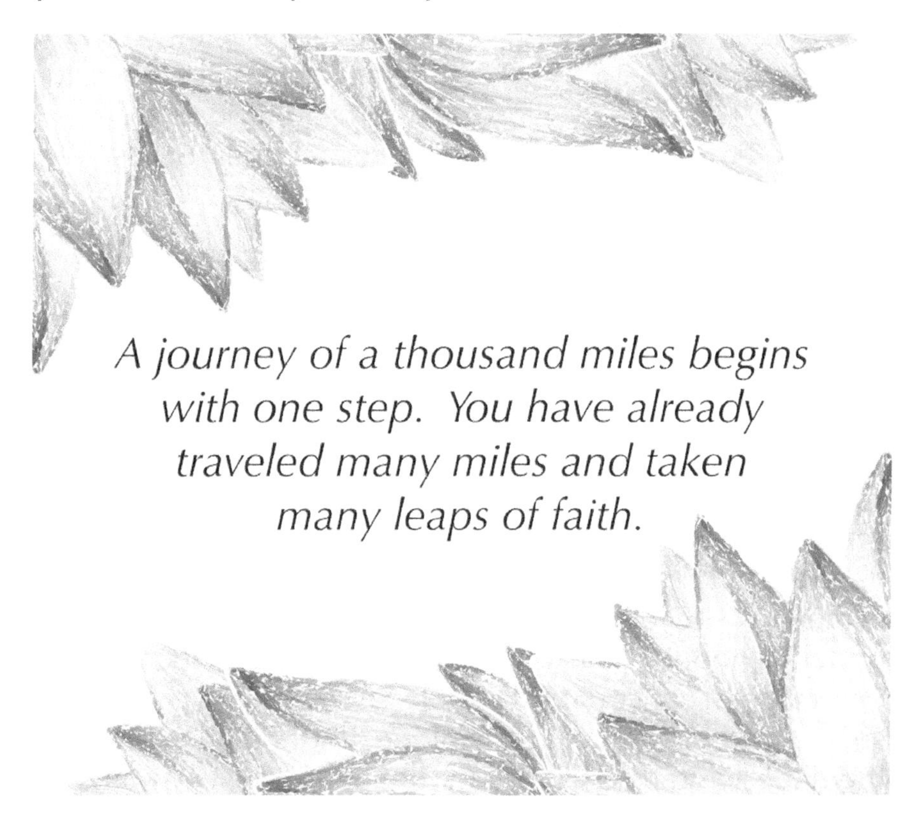

I invite you to step into the bullseye of your own Soul's Mastery.

Love,
Julia

About the Author

Julia Lewis is an Oracle for Souls. Her pursuit of her Spiritual Nature led her to this third chapter of her life. Her own Soul Mastery Journey empowered her to create this healing method that reveals and removes people's obstacles to the full expression of their life's purpose. Now they too can gain unrestricted access to their Soul's Mastery talents they were born with.

She is a retired Doctor of Chiropractic. She graduated Cum Laude in 1992 and practiced in San Jose, California until 2019. She started doing energetic healing in 1993 soon after she began her Chiropractic practice. She was aware of the unspoken, energetic connection that her intention and focus directed.

After having a near death experience in 1999 she dived deeper studying numerous healing techniques. She often achieved teacher level status to not only improve her patient's health, it also awakened her Soul's Mastery Skills. She practiced gentle, non-force adjusting and specialized in energetic techniques that helped resolve the underlying causes for emotional upsets, hormonal imbalances, allergies, arthritis, asthma, autoimmune conditions, chronic pain, fatigue, insomnia and more.

Her first career was in television production. She started working full time at a TV station in Corpus Christi, Texas during her senior year of high school. Four years later she got her dream job at WRC/NBC in Washington, DC. She worked in the studio as a camera operator and in production doing electronic graphics. After 11 years she had a buyout opportunity that allowed her to shift careers and attend Life Chiropractic College in Marietta, Georgia.

She is the oldest of four children and grew up in San Antonio and Corpus Christi, Texas.

Julia & brother

Richard and Julia

Connie, Julia, & Mom

Chiropractic Graduation

Julia's Chiropractic office

Julia with Wings

The End

The Beginning
SoulMasteryJourney.com

Made in the USA
Las Vegas, NV
13 April 2023